A CERTAIN EMANCIPATION OF WOMEN

Dear Bruce,

Vive la France!

Thank you so much for your support + interest. I look forward to your erudite critique!

Warmly,

Tracy

A CERTAIN EMANCIPATION OF WOMEN

Gender, Citizenship, and the *Causes Célèbres* of Eighteenth-Century France

Tracey Rizzo

SUP

Selinsgrove: Susquehanna University Press

Associated University Presses
2010 Eastpark Boulevard
Cranbury, NJ 08512

The paper used in this publication meets the requirements of the American National Standard for Permanence of Paper for Printed Library Materials Z39.48–1984.

Library of Congress Cataloging-in-Publication Data

Rizzo, Tracey.
A certain emancipation of women : gender, citizenship, and the causes célèbres of eighteenth-century France / Tracey Rizzo.
p. cm.
Includes bibliographical references (p.) and index.
ISBN 1-57591-087-X (alk. paper)
1. Women—Legal status, laws, etc.—France—Cases. 2. Women's rights—France—History—18th century. I. Title.
KJV332.R59 2004
342.7308'78'09033—dc22

2004007337

PRINTED IN THE UNITED STATES OF AMERICA

Contents

Acknowledgments

As this project has evolved over many years I have incurred many debts. Original research was conducted in 1989/90 thanks to a Fulbright grant which enabled a year's residence in Paris. Thanks to my graduate advisor, Raymond Birn, I had the good fortune of shaping the contours of the project in conversations with French scholars of his acquaintance: Arlette Farge, Roger Chartier, and Daniel Roche. This work continues to bear the marks of Ray's insights and expertise. I also thank Julie Paulsen and Raja Abusharr for research assistance in Paris. Subsequent trips to Paris were funded by Furman University and UNC-Asheville; I am enormously grateful for that support. Back on this side of the Atlantic, a number of scholars and friends have commented on earlier versions of the manuscript. I especially thank Barbara Corrado Pope, William Duvall, Carol Blum, Dale van Kley, and Judith Zinsser. Of all my debts, I owe the greatest thanks to Jeffrey Merrick without whose encouragement this project would not have achieved fruition. His peerless knowledge of the subject, willingness to entertain dialogue for nearly 10 years now, and persistent disagreement with my thesis (!) has deepened my thinking. For secretarial support I thank Jo Steininger, and for editorial support the staff at Associated University Presses and at Susquehanna University Press. Their commissioned reader's insightful comments made this version of the work much stronger. Guest editor of the Apple Zimmerman series in Early Modern Culture, Carole Levin, is much appreciated for encouraging my interest in the Susquehanna University Press. This book owes its completion to my chair at UNCA, Grant Hardy, who has provided material and moral support over the years. Finally, and most importantly, I thank my husband Kenneth Banks. For ten years now, our research trips, exchanges of manuscripts, and table talk have facilitated my professional growth in immeasurable ways. But even more than his brilliance as a historian, I appreciate his generosity as a friend and life partner who has helped to create a life where work and family are mutually supporting, without which no creativity can fluorish.

A CERTAIN EMANCIPATION OF WOMEN

Introduction

> Without a doubt, it is personal greatness which brings virtue and ennobles every social condition; and if you will only use virtue to efface the shameful circumstances of your birth [the fruit of adultery], your conduct will bring you glory, and we ourselves will applaud so much courage, and, touched by your situation, our beneficence will soften it.[1]

In 1784, Toulousan lawyer Janoles assured a woman born of an adulterous affair in Nîmes that she could overcome the prejudices attached to her status by her personal conduct. Even though Elisabeth Emerie lost her bid for a share in her mother's inheritance because her birth mother was discovered to be a dressmaker and occasional prostitute, her lawyer guaranteed her the indulgence of the law and the state, if she, of her own merits, proved herself virtuous. An account of the case appeared in *Les Causes célèbres, curieuses et intéressantes de toutes les cours souveraines du Royaume avec les jugements qui les ont décidées,* edited by Nicolas Toussaint le Moyne Des Essarts and published in Paris between 1773 and 1789. With a keen eye on the literary marketplace, Des Essarts, himself a lawyer, suspected that representations of court cases, especially sentimental tales of the intimate lives of ordinary people, would become bestsellers. As became standard in the ninety-eight volumes and 695 cases which comprised it, Des Essarts' account of a case included lengthy quotes from lawyers whose rhetoric he favored and a basic retelling of the case.

Therein, lawyers like Janoles and editors like Des Essarts called for the liberation of women from tyrannical fathers, abusive husbands, public opinion, and even oppressive laws, like that maintaining the stigma of illegitimacy, in the dozens of seductions, separations, rapes, and infanticides on which this study is based. Thus, *A Certain Emancipation of Women* exposes a liberatory moment, an opening, in which late eighteenth-century constructions of female citizenship offered virtuous women, regardless of rank or even race, "strategic possibilities" for establishing modern identities—defined as self-creating, autonomous, and capable of moral judgement and reason.[2] Instead of being excluded from *vir*tue, women from a variety of social classes, and from the provinces and the Caribbean colonies, are represented in the *Causes célèbres* as exemplars, more independent from the particularistic interests, derived from class status and personal ambition, which govern the actions of the men who oppress them.[3]

This moment was possible for several related reasons. The late eighteenth century saw, first, the influence of the Enlightenment on lawyers and magistrates especially in terms of natural law whose ascendancy enabled a widespread reevaluation of family law and custom; second, the apotheosis of critiques of paternal and monarchial power which had implications for women's status; third, a cult of *sensibilité* in which women (as authors, readers, and theatergoers) actively participated in the construction of virtuous identities, especially in the context of the emergence of the sentimental melodrama.

In the *Causes célèbres*, hundreds of women won their court cases in the 1770s and 1780s as their lawyers represented them in heartrending language as embodiments of tormented virtue. *A Certain Emancipation of Women* describes how the discourse of virtue, articulated in the novels but also the law courts and philosophical treatises of the second half of the eighteenth century, actually benefitted French women on the threshold of modernity. While some recent works explore the degree to which shifting representations of virtue benefitted women,[4] more specialized studies of lived experience also indicate a "certain emancipation of women." For example, Alain Lottin and G. Savelon found in their exhaustive study of separation suits an "increase in female demands at the end of the century (6 to 1) [which] perhaps testifies to a certain emancipation of women. The percentage of mutual demands also doubled."[5] Yet rarely do these two enterprises intersect. Few scholars have attempted to demonstrate the means by which representations both reflect and transform the lives of historical actors. This study offers a rare opportunity to glimpse that intersection as the *Causes célèbres* merges representations and lived experience, fact and fiction.

A spate of recent scholarship, continuing a decades' long conversation, explores visual and textual representations of virtue during the late eighteenth century, including the Revolution.[6] Indeed, some scholars conclude that these representations actually eroded women's position by the end of the century. Jeffrey Merrick and Nadine Berenguier contend that though individual women won their cases in court, "the female sex as a whole lost" because lawyers did not press for more general improvements in women's condition and because their defense rested on limiting stereotypes.[7] Such a conclusion demonstrates the necessity for an explication of the *Causes célèbres* as a whole, for the magnitude of change is only visible after reviewing hundreds of defense strategies involving a wide variety of clients, their lawyers, and civil cases. By examining representations of virtue in the context of lived experience, one that is more complex than can be described by the phrases "cult of domesticity" or "separate spheres," it is clear that a shift in mentality had taken place that would not be eradicated by late revolutionary legislative decrees and the Napoleonic Code.

Another strand of relevant scholarship debates the degree to which women were able to demonstrate eligibility for citizenship during the Revolution. According to Joan Wallach Scott, contestation and contradiction inhere in the western construct of modern individualism; these "paradoxes" are especially evident when considering "female citizenship" since citizenship is an inherently masculine construct.[8] Carla Hesse, on the other hand, offers a less radical critique of modernity's formative period, alleging that women's exclusion was based on a prejudice that they were incapable of "reasoning about general rather than particular interest."[9] While both scholars describe the processes by which women were excluded from citizenship, they also reveal the degree to which individual French women during and after the Revolution challenged that exclusion. By expanding the conversation backwards into the 1770s and 1780s, I intend to show that such challenges were enabled by an Enlightenment discourse on virtue that in fact attributed to women the capacity for modern individualism precisely to the degree that they were seen as less self-interested than men.

Thus it is possible, indeed necessary, to maintain two mutually exclusive propositions at once. By the end of the Enlightenment, a discourse engaged by lawyers, philosophes, novelists, and others enabled women to establish modern identities as reasonable individuals capable of citizenship. But also, by the end of the Enlightenment, specifically during the radical phase of the Revolution, such possibilities were foreclosed by the masculinist prejudices of Jacobins and later revolutionaries who called for separate spheres as a reaction to the explosion of women's participation in public life from 1789 on.[10] Thus a narrative of women's empowerment, derived from their possession of virtue, interacts with a counter-narrative of women's disempowerment, derived from their subservience to public opinion which confers honor.

Sources of Women's Empowerment

In such novels as Rousseau's *La Nouvelle Heloïse,* virtue eclipsed honor in eighteenth-century discourses, as Marisa Linton has recently documented. While honor was traditionally associated with rank, virtue was distinct in its independence from public opinion, custom, and privilege: it resided, innately, in the individual. Moreover, as exemplified in Rousseau's "Julie," "the virtuous woman was empowered to speak out against the false expectations of noble honor."[11] Real life "Julies" spoke out in many a "cause célèbre" as well, manifesting their virtue through their degree of self-sacrifice and immunity to the passions as they challenged the preoccupations with family name and lineage that brought domestic matters to court.

Des Essarts, too, offered readers a "Julie," in his play of 1784, *Emile et Sophie, ou les époux désunis.* Preoccupied with marital breakdown (no issue brought more women before the magistracy in the *Causes célèbres*), Des Essarts described a simple provincial couple and their son whose bliss was destroyed by their migration to Paris, "this infamous asylum of vice and corruption" in which the "adorable wife" became debauched and a "most vile" creature. Sophie was the "living image of virtue" before her "fall" at the hands of a scoundrel, about whom little is revealed. Though she insists upon her innocence, she prefers death to Emile's scorn, pleading: "listen to me or I will die of misery at your feet," if not for herself, then for the sake of their son. They reconcile after a letter from a seducer (rapist?), "the infamous author of all of my troubles," finally convinces Emile of her innocence. The curtain closes on their embrace amidst a torrent of mutually shed tears.[12] Sophie's persistent virtue acquitted her of any taint of shame, and in the context of domestic bliss she is redeemed.

In the cult of *sensibilité* inheres the democratic possibilities of melodrama.[13] Weeping together over sentimental tales of tormented virtue, men and women, aristocrat and bourgeois, participated equally in this aspect of *prerevolutionary*, late-eighteenth-century culture. The *Causes célèbres* contains hundreds of stories of tormented virtue that were intended to evoke torrents of tears. So even though "Women and dependents were factually and legally excluded from the political public sphere, ... female readers as well as apprentices and servants often took a more active part in the literary public sphere than the owners of private property and family heads themselves."[14] Jürgen Habermas equates the literary sphere with the political one, indicating that women still retained one point of entry into public life: print. As readers and subjects, as representations and as historical actors, but more directly as authors and consumers, women actively participated in the discourse on virtue, demanding satisfaction when wronged and setting precedents for broader changes to be accomplished later.

Because honor was traditionally associated with rank, virtue was distinct in its independence from public opinion, custom, and privilege: it resided, innately, in the individual.[15] Class and gender differentials were streamlined in the late eighteenth century, and competing codes of honor—which were often at the root of a *cause célèbre*—became subsumed under two—the first, perhaps the more complex, associated with the public sphere (principally, but not exclusively, masculine), and the second for the private (principally, but not exclusively, feminine). In reality, these spheres intersected in many women's experience. For example, Des Essarts defended the professional integrity and honor of a midwife accused of botching a Cesarean in Sedan in 1775, when in fact it was a male apprentice who performed the operation. Des Essarts applauded the midwife's reluctance to perform an operation which "jeopardizes the mother's life. The life of the mother is more precious than that of the infant: she is already a citizen, she has been useful. Everyone around her owes her their happiness, and often their virtue."[16] This language, already prevalent in 1775, illustrates the degree to which the evolving discourse on citizenship featured virtue and the means by which virtuous women would establish their citizenship.

Thus even the poor rural woman was essential to society to the degree she imparted virtue to those around her. Above the self-interest which preoccupied the powerful, she was more likely to embody virtue. Others would have to eschew their former claims to honor, based on rank or status, to realize virtue. In a case involving misalliance, Des Essarts describes the disowned noble who learns a lesson: "he discovered that the charms of mediocrity and the consolations of virtue are not always frivolous chimeras of the imagination."[17] Virtue, then, is what truly ennobles, and preoccupations with aristocratic honor were seen as increasingly anachronistic. Writes Sarah Maza: "Starting in the 1760s, educated members of the aristocracy sought to redefine the claims of their class to leadership of the nation by grounding them in utilitarian categories such as merit, virtue, or *bienfaisance*, instead of blood-lines and privilege."[18]

Only individual inalterable virtue, independent of a public opinion which could be prone to error, could merit citizenship. Rendering individuals transparent through melodramatic depictions of their suffering so that their virtue would be manifest became the goal of lawyers and culminated in the Republic of Virtue. The *Causes célèbres* is foundational to this process. According to Maza, lawyers, like those arguing "causes célèbres," "sought to create an unmediated connection between the presumed virtue and sensibility of their client and that of their readers. . . . This rhetorical strategy points to the most ominous development of the Revolution, the Jacobin reign of Virtue and Terror."[19] At the same time, precedents for revolutionary legislation on family law, —divorce, adoption, illegitimacy—much of it progressive and most of which endured beyond the Revolution (albeit sometimes in altered forms)can be found in the court cases of the 1770s and 1780s, all of this located in the theatrical and melodramatic discourse prevalent in popular reading material of the time.

Sources of Women's Disempowerment

Even as progressive legislation was passed to the benefit of women, debates about citizenship during the Revolution explicitly disempowered them. "Male legislators thus passed laws with a contradictory effect on women, rendering them both objects of legislative concern and subjects with civil rights." Scott continues to describe the paradox in which women were recognized as "civil agents," but then excluded from politics.[20] This schizophrenia about women's civil status, especially prominent during the Republic of Virtue, ironically sustains the liberatory moment. So even as Jacobins curbed women's political activism in the mid 1790s, Patrice Higonnet writes of the potential of Jacobinism to foster women's emancipation: "Jacobins were (unknowing) Kantians, promoting universally acceptable behavior for every man and woman." And, more specifically, "the more thoughtful Jacobins," like Condorcet and Sièyes, "understood that equality of the sexes followed from their ideals."[21] Yet this "minoritarian" position was not sufficient to prevent the majority from calling for separate spheres, limiting women's "citizenship" to childrearing.

The Jacobin zeal for confining women to the private sphere had its roots in the writings of Rousseau, precursors to the Republic of Virtue *and* the cult of domesticity. According to Rousseau, "A home whose mistress is absent is a body without a soul which soon falls into corruption; a woman outside of her home loses her greatest luster, and, despoiled of her real ornaments, she displays herself indecently. . . . Whatever she may do, one feels in public she is not in her place. . . ."[22] Like the nation, the home was also described metaphorically as a body, a body, moreover which loses its integrity when its most important member abandons it.

Two distinct approaches characterize Rousseau's program for confining women. On the one hand, he advocated forcing their confinement and acclimating them to obedience and servitude from childhood:

> Girls must be thwarted early in life. This misfortune, if it is a misfortune for them, is inseparable from their sex—they must become accustomed to constraint so that it does not bother them. They must subdue all their own fantasies to the will of others. . . . It is just that

> this sex share the difficulties it has caused in us. Do not permit them an instant of their lives free from bondage.[23]

Des Essarts also wrote that boys and girls should be raised differently in order to train them to effectively perform their appropriate roles. Yet he believed that these roles need only be encouraged; nature determined that males would command and females would obey. In a child abuse case he explained: "In general, girls are more docile than boys; nature has wisely established this difference between the sexes: one must command while the other must always obey. It is therefore necessary to accustom girls to an extreme docility from an early age."[24]

Rousseau's other approach, again for which parallels can be found in the *Causes célèbres*, includes the propagation of images of virtuous and sentimental women that appealed to female readers like Manon Roland; the whole cult of sentimentality exalted women's emotive capacities. As Carol Blum points out, these two approaches are not mutually exclusive: "the context of sentimental virtue served to ward off the image of the seductive and therefore controlling woman."[25] After mitigating their power over men, Rousseau compensated women with the idea that in domestic sweetness they would be adored by their husbands, children, and the state, and that by performing their naturally ordained roles they would prove themselves virtuous. He limited their function to reproduction and early child-rearing, and exalted both their capacity for this and its importance to the state in the form of "repopulation." His thoughts on breast-feeding are well known, but are exemplary enough to warrant repeating here: "Let mothers deign to nurse their babies, morals will reform themselves, feelings of nature will reawaken in all hearts, the state will be repopulated."[26]

Controlling women and achieving the decline of the aristocracy were two republican goals which coalesced in a pronounced hostility towards "effeminacy." The reluctance to breast-feed was seen to be a uniquely aristocratic corruption: republicans would remake the oversexed bodies of noblewomen. Joan Landes describes how republicans despised the fashionable society of the aristocracy and the concomitant freedom it provided women, claiming that both groups' "effeminacy" was ruining the nation. This fostered the "angry protest of those who celebrated virile constitutions of republics and despised the 'effeminized' status of men under absolutism."[27] Thus the ascension of virtue is also due to the masculine power it carries in its etymology—*vir*tue is produced only under *vir*ile republics.

Apropos of Republican Rome's ruin, Rousseau asked, "What are these effeminate ways?" proposing in its stead Sparta, where virtue "was now equated with military masculinity."[28] Not merely nostalgic for the past, revolutionaries, and Rousseau before them, made plans for a new republic based on the Spartan model. For Poland, Rousseau urged: "Let us tolerate military luxury, the luxury of weapons, of horses, but let all feminine finery be held in contempt."[29]

These sentiments were also expressed in the *Causes célèbres*. In a "cause célèbre" of 1785, lawyer Veyrier opened his case against a "widow accused of dissolute behavior during the year of mourning" accordingly:

> One sex has glorified itself while defaming the other; the weakest has usurped power by dint of weakness: the austere morality of our ancestors is now nothing more than a source of ridicule, and the fear of ridicule is our only modesty. Is it true, gentlemen, that severe morals are only a republican necessity? that they are useless or fatal to the constitution of an empire, after having carried Sparta and ancient Rome to the pinnacle of splendor? that honor, that principle behind every monarchy, is independent of virtue? that a depraved nation can be full of honor?[30]

In Veyrier's rhetoric a dramatic shift has occurred. Honor, now no longer defined as that which belonged only to men of noble birth, having been recently attached to the woman of good reputation, was now seen as an essentially masculine attribute. It then becomes virtue, a more perfect form of honor because innate and unalterable. This particular definition of honor is one which would achieve predominance during the Revolution. Such virtue could only be attained in the republican environments of Sparta and Rome, an attribute of men, spoiled by shameless women. Only women who accepted the cult of domesticity would be allowed membership in a civil society modeled after the great republics of antiquity in which women were more literally confined to the private sphere.

Yet, it was the concomitant separation of spheres that ultimately foreclosed the Republic of Virtue. The gendered designation of public and private entailed an access to privacy that was inimical to virtue because it precluded transparency. Moreover, this access to the private, this space made for dissimulation, was the women's sphere. And in the face of dissimulation there can be no virtue, only a kind of honor which becomes a mere concern with one's reputation and the use of artifice to maintain that reputation. This tension between transparancy and dissimulation animates all of the following cases.

Thus women achieved emancipation through favorable court verdicts and progressive legislation even as strands of radical thought founded modern cultural constructs which limited women's direct access to public life and political expression during and after the Revolution.

Paradoxes

Negotiating narrative and counternarrative, French feminists have struggled to construct modern identities ever since. Recourse to the state is one of their strategies and the role of the state in enabling access and even in designating honor and virtue evolved out of this liberatory moment when enlightened father-magistrates wrested control of family matters from self-interested men. That laws must protect honor, especially tormented female honor, is argued throughout the *Causes célèbres.* This empowers the state to determine status rather than custom, tradition, rank, or class, resulting in an egalitarianism which Des Essarts articulated in 1783:

> In France, all men are of the same blood; they are all free and perfectly equal from this point of view; they are all equally eligible for every honor and distinction which merit or fortune can procure; there is no one who cannot aspire to them; the difference in conditions is reconciled, in this spirit, by this equality; and however abject the origin of a citizen, [prejudices] disappear regarding his descendants by the hard-earned distinctions which erase them.[31]

This was the case with Elisabeth Emerie who was assured the indulgence of the law despite the fact that she was illegitimate. By the time of the Terror, these principles were combined to enforce a paradoxical egalitarianism in which all become equal in their subservience to the state. But the Terror was only one outcome of the "certain emancipation" emerging in the 1780s.

The possibility of obtaining esteem through the possession of honor was a seductive proposition; meeting a standard of behavior was something, in theory at least, that all could do as long as they could submit their self-interest to the public good. "Prejudices disappear" in a world in which virtue trumps honor. In the following chapters, I will read the competition between particularistic conceptions of honor as the first cause of case after case and argue that such debates facilitated the shift to a more universal virtue.

Chapter one, an exploration of the *Causes célèbres* as source, opens with an account of adultery which led to murder. A preoccupation with family name motivated an arranged and loveless marriage which left the spouses vulnerable to the passions. When the husband became involved with another woman, her preoccupation with his honor precluded their escape to another country. When *his* preoccupation with *her* honor inspired an obsession with legitimizing their union, he became homicidal. He explained: "Led on by a violent passion, even by an excess of honor, I found myself a criminal though I only believed myself virtuous."[32] Des Essarts' inclusion of the case indicates the multiple functions of his tome: indulgence of sensibility, exposition of moderation, and portrayal of the complex meanings of honor and virtue. Disentangling the complex motives of the participants in this drama, chapter one explains why the *Causes célèbres* is a peerless source for such an explication.

In chapter two, I explore three cases of seduction in which the authority of fathers is called into question. In the first, a young noble seduces a virtuous bourgeoise with his egalitarian rhetoric. When his father intervenes to halt this misalliance, Barère de Vieuzac, future regicide, represented the abandoned spouse in the ensuing trial and issued an appeal that condemned the self-interestedness of the father as well as aristocratic hegemony. A libertine aristocrat is the antagonist in the second case, featured here for its usefulness in depicting the clash of aristocratic notions of honor with those of his "victim," a social inferior whom he has seduced and abandoned. Attenuating still more of the patriarchal hierarchy, lawyers challenged paternal authority in general as they argued cases involving litigants from a variety of socioeconomic classes. In the third case, a petite bourgeois father is challenged by his determined daughter and her forbidden lover. Because she was pregnant, the defense lawyer urged the court to grant the child full legitimacy by overruling the obstructionist father who would not permit a marriage between the lovers. He depicted marriage as a Rousseauian union based on mutual sympathy, a natural union, a microcosm of the social contract. These cases set precedents for legislation ending discrimination against the "illegitimate," and the tradition of arranged marriages, thus limiting paternal authority.

In the *Causes célèbres* still more radical claims were advanced by lawyers disputing male authority as women won their suits for separation. Husbands who proved themselves unworthy of partnership with a virtuous woman were ostracized by lawyers and magistrates. Chapter three features two such cases and will show how defense lawyers promoted the independence of women from morally—and sometimes financially—bankrupt husbands. In these cases, the courts determined that educated and virtuous women should not have to endure either physical or psychological abuse from their husbands. "Mental cruelty" was admitted as a cause for granting separation, as was "character assassination." A husband who had wrongly charged his wife with adultery, for example, thus delivering a significant blow to her reputation, had neglected to safeguard her honor, his chief duty; he thereby ceded any claims he had had to her allegiance and could no longer be called her "husband" at all. In the third case, a bride and groom, forced into a marriage they despised by their fathers, allege that their marriage was never consummated and that it must be annulled. Bearing the child of another man, demoiselle Alliot sought the legal freedom to marry her lover. Obstructing her in this case was neither her father (whose cruelty had been softened by her more indulgent mother), nor her erstwhile first "husband," but a mysterious stranger, known only as a "bourgeois de Paris," who claimed to be representing "public order" or the common good. Wicked father, disinterested husband, and licentious aristocratic woman—all are attacked in the name of some higher principle—the integrity of citizenship which could only be guaranteed in unions grounded in virtuous procreation.

The cases in chapter four revolve around the conception of children and the intervention of the state to clarify parentage. However, aristocratic libertinage is not the cause of illegitimacy here; rather it is rape. In one, a young petite bourgeoise dies after the rapist and father of her child libels her by alleging she was a prostitute. Des Essarts claims it was public opinion that dealt the final, fatal blow to her broken heart. In another, a textile worker was accused by townspeople of infanticide when they discovered her stillborn child. It was none other than Barère de Vieuzac who proved her innocence as he condemned the tyranny of public opinion. He appealed to the court's inclination to believe in the inevitable and unchanging quality of maternal tenderness; for him infanticide was always already precluded. This defense, based on sentimental maternity and natural law, resulted in the acquittal of all the accused infanticides in the *Causes célèbres*, regardless of the circumstances which resulted in pregnancy. Thus, even those women whose illegitimate pregnancies were voluntary benefitted from this liberatory moment, suggesting that a relative freedom from the tyranny of public opinion and the "clamor of a misguided people" enabled women to achieve a measure of autonomy. And unlike the bourgeois women who constitute the majority of the litigants in the cases discussed in the prior chapters, these women are poor, suggesting that social status was not always the principal determinant of verdicts.

Focused on the constructive period of the 1780s, this book only glimpses the Revolutionary period in its conclusion. A brief analysis of Des Essarts' account of the trial of Manon Roland, executed in 1793 for her role in an alleged Girondist conspiracy, reveals the consistency of his representations of virtue across two decades despite dramatically changed circumstances. The degree to which this revolutionary heroine was in fact virtuous is explored by Des Essarts who demonstrates an ambivalence about her actions in the political sphere. As Chantal Thomas puts it: "The women of 1789 [including Roland] were set before a classic double bind: remain women, but deny themselves all exaltation and all heroic action, or else attain the sublime, but transgress the ideal reserved for their sex."[33] Though her trial had little to do with family matters, her identity was constructed by supporters and opponents within the context of familial notions of women's virtue. A woman and a hero, at least according to Des Essarts, Roland, as a breast-feeding mother and disciple of Rousseau, embodied an ideal which emerged in the *Causes célèbres* of the 1770s and 1780s. Manifestly virtuous, she spoke her truth, tearing away the "masks which hid these terrifying assassins [Jacobins complicit in the September Massacres which took the lives of some 1200 Parisian prisoners]."[34] For this she met her fate at the scaffold, her liberatory moment permanently foreclosed.

By moving towards the era of the Republic of Virtue, I consider the possibilities, both realized and foreclosed, of the liberatory moment developed throughout. With aristocratic, paternal, and spousal authority questioned by the clever argumentation of lawyers as well as by a plethora of decisions handed down by courts, and with even public opinion roundly denounced by the law as fallible, the construction of women as modern citizens (self-creating, autonomous, and capable of moral judgement, reason, and virtue) was nearly complete. But as revolutionary events propelled more women into public action, the call for separate spheres grew louder. The contradictory tenets of the liberatory moment reached an impasse.

This is a book of origins. It could easily have been a book of outcomes, for just as some scholars situate the evolution of women into citizens in the context of the impending Revolution, others focus on the era of religious Reformation. And while it would be negligent to ignore the degree to which representations of gender roles in the *Causes célèbres* are outcomes of revisions in honor codes and defense strategies promulgated in the sixteenth and seventeenth centuries, that is not the primary concern of the present work. The proximity of the 1770s and 1780s to the 1790s is irresistible, especially when the ideas and even some of the personnel of the former period make their way quite literally into the latter. Yet the evolution of these representations through the 1790s does not amount to the only interpretation of their meaning. Narrative and counternarrative in this pivotal moment in the construction of modern women's identities do not lead exclusively to a negative outcome. A broader view is required.

1

The *Causes Célèbres*

If those who would abandon the empire of their hearts to ardent passions read this horrifying story, they will tremble with horror to see an honest man become a scoundrel in an instant. It is however love, this precious consolation of the human race, which made a virtuous and irreproachable citizen into a vile assassin and execrable henchman.[1]

THE TRANSFORMATION OF THE VIRTUOUS CITIZEN INTO A VILE ASSASSIN too frequently occurred under the Republic of Virtue: think only of Charlotte Corday motivated by an excess of self-righteousness to assassinate a political enemy. An excess of honor could also be ruinous, according to the murderer whose story opens this chapter, the retelling of which will provide an opportunity to consider the sometimes dangerous liaison between honor and virtue.

Des Essarts was a man of moderation; during the Revolution he was likely a Girondist sympathizer. He used his pen to preach moderation. He frequently and explicitly stated the didactic purpose behind his reportage of "causes célèbres" or, in this case "procès fameux." In his introductions to cases, he sometimes begged his readers' forgiveness, especially when details were "shameful" or "horrifying." He requested their indulgence as well; after all, he was only doing his civic duty by offering lessons in virtue, the account of a "cause célèbre" functioning as a deterrent:

> But it is our duty to remind those who would let themselves be mastered by ardent passions of all the dangers to which they expose themselves. The portrait of the horrible consequences of crime can stop a hand ready to follow a fatal impulse; it can conserve virtue in

> weak souls who are on the verge of becoming guilty; finally it can render virtue dearer. This is the goal we propose for ourselves, by demonstrating that criminals are always miserable even if they escape the punishment they deserve.[2]

On March 30, 1784, M——slit his wife's throat in order to be rid of her, thereby freeing himself to marry his mistress. Sympathetic towards this "unfortunate" criminal, Des Essarts used the case as a vehicle to emphasize the injustice of arranged marriages which leave people prey to violent passions, though parents think such marriages will have the opposite effect. The criminal himself blamed his parents for trying to "spare my youth from the dangers of passion." He tried to love his wife, and then later to suppress his unmet need for love, but, he goes on: "My heart, naturally 'sensible,' and up until then a stranger to love, became prey to all its furors."[3] The dangers of intense romantic love were one of the principal subtexts of the *Causes célèbres.* Des Essarts preached elsewhere: "Of all the passions, the one which brings the greatest effervescence to the senses of man is without a doubt love. If this passion in a virtuous and well-born soul can sometimes be the cause of the loveliest actions, it inspires only too often heinous crimes in corrupt hearts."[4]

As a "medico-philosophical literature" emerged in the Enlightenment, philosophes pondered the vulnerability of human beings to "degeneration." In particular, widely read theories of sensibility help us understand why M——expected his portrait of his heart as "naturally sensible" to exonerate him. Though normally a praiseworthy quality that drove "humankind's most basic and ethical responses," overdeveloped or misdirected sensibility could "induce physical frailty, moral perversion, and even hereditary degeneration." Thus by the 1770s, according to Anne Vila, "the ambiguity of vital sensibility seemed so acute that a redefinition of the property was virtually inevitable." One aspect of this redefinition was the articulation of a sexually dimorphous model in which women or too highly refined men were thought more prone to heightened sensibility.[5]

Unable to love his wife, M——was involved with his mistress for four years in what Des Essarts alleged can only be called a "dangerous liaison." When her family found out and disowned her, he advocated flight to another country but she refused, not wanting to dishonor her beloved's good aristocratic name.

In spite of his prestigious lineage, this criminal, whose name Des Essarts never revealed ("out of respect for the unfortunate parents of this scoundrel"), demonstrated his commitment to virtue and good citizenship. He described what motivated him to commit this heinous crime in the first place: "Led on by a violent passion, even by an excess of honor, I found myself a criminal though I only believed myself virtuous."[6] Moreover, another excessive love, that of France, motivated M——'s next move. After the murder, he fled to another country, exclaiming: "Alas! It is not as a Frenchman that I am guilty! It is not her people who I have offended." He knew that he must pay for these excesses with his life, but he begged the queen of his self-imposed place of exile not to return him to France. When she, ignoring his protests, decided to comply with his extradition orders, he killed himself on June 17, 1785, preferring suicide in a foreign land to the disgrace of a public execution in his beloved France.

Though not usually ending in death, conflicts between honor and virtue, self-sacrifice and self-interest, motivated many "causes célèbres" and enabled Des Essarts and the lawyers he quoted to moralize. Especially preponderant in the collection, new mandates, like those arising from M——'s case, for the instructing and molding of citizens were not only issued in increasing numbers by lawyers, but were heard by the large population of urban and provincial readers who subscribed to the journal.

According to reviews by the leading literary journals of the day, women as well as men "avidly read" and "learned by heart" tearjerkers in the *Causes célèbres* which, unlike similar enterprises of the sixteenth and seventeenth centuries, introduced complex modes of emplotment, and were more melodramatic than the "nouvelles" approach used in earlier collections.[7] Lamoignon Malesherbes, secretary of state for Louis XVI, wrote as early as 1774: "Has anyone reflected on the gradual progress that printed memoirs have had on minds over the past 20 years? Women who once read only novels now read them."[8] Des Essarts knew that women read his cases because whenever "shameful" details had to be disclosed (sex acts, genitals, etc.), he used Latin, "a language unknown to persons of the sex in whom modesty is so easily alarmed."

Des Essarts even trumpeted the utility of his collection for female readers:

> In this collection, we have given several examples of seductions and of punishments inflicted by the tribunals. We do not hesitate to multiply these examples; they are so many lessons for the female sex who can learn how they should be on guard against seduction, and how succumbing should never be at the cost of a legitimate union. It is only then that their fecundity is honorable, that they supremely enjoy the sweetness of love and maternity, and have the glory of forming subjects for religion and citizens for the state.[9]

Women's access to citizenship then is through child rearing, and their honor, if not their virtue, resides in the appropriate use of their bodies. While this formulation can be read as a paternalistic justification for confining women to domesticity, it also underscores the means by which women could develop modern identities as they are appealed to as sensible and reasonable readers capable of being "on guard" against seduction, capable of controlling access to their bodies.

Didactic motives inspired other chroniclers of court cases in the eighteenth century, most of whom focused on contemporary cases, though the earliest of them, Gayot de Pitaval, included famous cases from antiquity through the seventeenth century. That approach had lost its appeal by the time Des Essarts began publication—so much so that he apologized to his readers for including a case from 1729, assuring them that "the singularity of this case will certainly excuse its antiquity. Though it is not recent, it is not less piquant, and consequently deserves to be ranked among the most curious cases."[10] And curious it was, debating the legitimacy of a transvestite's will.

Above all, Des Essarts preferred to offer his readers "recent events which take place during our time, and perhaps under our very own eyes" and "our own history of the generation with whom we live."[11] Moreover, the lives of the great were seldom of interest to him, devoid as they were, perhaps ironically, of opportunities for moral edification:

> The history of each nation ordinarily offers only the grand traits which characterize the vices and virtues of Princes, of their generals, their favorites: it disdains depicting the morals and private lives of society's inferior classes. The great crimes of Nations, their misfortunes, their vengeful acts, events which astonish the imagination, or which influence the fate of governments, these are the facts which

> constitute the annals of Empires, and which attract the historian's attention; one must believe that [historians] write only for a very small number of readers, and that the rest of the human race does not exist for them.[12]

Though historians write for a rarified minority, journalists like Des Essarts aimed at the masses on the premise that people would enjoy reading about people like themselves, especially when their messy private lives became public knowledge. Indeed, such cases attracted large numbers of readers. It is necessary to explore diverse ways of indicating the popularity of the *Causes célèbres* because of the absence of subscription lists or other publishers' records. A perusal of death inventories, for example, reveals that the important Parisian editors Cavelier, Estienne, and Durand all possessed collections of *Causes célèbres,* though not those of Des Essarts. Des Essarts' collection was found in the inventory of Louis Muget, proprietor of a reading room in Valence; in his library they were shelved next to France's most popular journals. Another indicator of popularity is the existence of counterfeit editions which were printed in Avignon, a fact which both annoyed and pleased Des Essarts: "Two editions made of this journal and several counterfeits in foreign countries indicate the receptivity of the public, and the success of the work."[13]

Surely, more people read them than subscribed to them, since, as Roger Chartier has shown, many texts were read in libraries and private reading rooms in this period, public reading rivalling private ownership as an indicator of readership.[14] Launching his new enterprise in 1786, the *Procès fameux,* Des Essarts could be confident of success because "the *Causes célèbres* is in all the libraries."[15] Friedrich Schiller, in his 1774 preface to the German translation of Des Essarts' collaborator, François Richer's *Causes célèbres,* praised its modernity for just this reason: it introduced the possibility, in Lüsebrink's paraphrasing, for "an enlightened mass literature."[16]

Thus readership of the *Causes célèbres* was inclusive of both genders as well as of literate urban and provincial readers from a variety of social classes. Because the market for them was so large, other editors peddled their own versions of "causes célèbres." Between 1734 and 1789, seven different editors compiled nine collections in twenty-three editions totaling 253 volumes and over 1500 cases.[17] Until the 1770s these collections enjoyed what Lüsebrink calls a quasi-monopoly of the market for court cases. However, in that decade, as an attestation to their popularity, a veritable explosion of *causes célèbres* occurred in journals and gazettes, many of the most fashionable now adding permanent sections devoted to the presentation of *causes célèbres.* By 1786 even the Paris press lord Charles-Joseph Panckoucke included "Causes célèbres" in the title of his new literary review.[18] Lüsebrink cites contemporary journals which provide abundant testimony to this fact: "*L'Année Littéraire* spoke of the stunning success of the *Causes célèbres* 'avidly read,' which was perpetuated for as many as forty years after the first edition. . . . *La Gazette Universelle de Littérature,* le *Journal Encyclopédique,* and la *Gazette et Avant-Coureur de Littérature* equally expressed their admiration of the numbers of subscriptions and sales of the *Causes célèbres* of Richer and of Des Essarts."[19]

Such references suggest the types of people who read the *Causes célèbres.* What types of people were featured therein? Who were these ordinary people that everyone wanted to read about, and what issues brought them before the magistracy?

I have selected 223 cases out of the collection which involve both male and female litigants. These are the principal topics covered in those cases:

Seductions/Rapes	34
Validity of marriages	24
Illegitimate children	20
Separations	19
Inheritance disputes	17
Murders	16
Adultery	10
Demands for food	10
Parricides	7
Infanticides	7
Bigamy	6
Impotence	5
Charivari	5
Male authority	5
Medical abuses	5
Incest	2

The numbers may not add up, some cases defying categorization, others crossing over into more than one category. But numbers, themselves, can be revealing. The infrequency of incest, for example, suggests not that this offense was rarely committed, but that it was unlikely to be brought before the magistrates. Adultery also appears to have occurred with a surprising infrequency, but the numbers hide the fact that it was often a cause for separation. These figures reveal more about Des Essarts' editorial strategies than the actual commissions of crimes or the frequency with which such issues were presented in court.

I have also identified the location in which the incident took place, which is not necessarily the same place where the case was tried. More incidents occurred in small towns or villages than in Paris (28 as compared to 27). Others took place in towns that held the seats of parlement: 9 in Toulouse, 4 in Bordeaux, and 3 each in Nancy, Grenoble, and Rouen. Three also occurred in Lyons. Nine more occurred in foreign countries. His inclusion of foreign cases suggests a taste for the exotic, which he no doubt shared with his readers, and provided opportunities to compare the customs and laws of different countries as well as those of France's overseas colonies, especially Saint-Domingue.

A statistical analysis of 96 of these cases (selected from a larger random sampling on the basis of complete information) enables an analysis of the backgrounds of the litigants. There are 17 cases in which both parties are nobles, 7 involving what might be called the grande bourgeoisie, 26 bourgeois proper (in 2 of these, one litigant was bourgeois, the other noble), 17 artisans and well-off peasants, and 23 poor, either urban or rural (in 3 of these, one of the litigants was noble). Des Essarts was more interested in telling the stories of the less privileged, the combined totals of the lower classes numbering half again as many as the class from which he came—the bourgeoisie proper: it was the petite bourgeoisie that interested him most, and he featured stories which pitted them against corrupt nobles.

The following chapters, organized by incident, illustrate how these groups were linked with various types of cases, showing for example, that few of the murder cases involved nobles, but that nobles dominated most of the separations and inheritance disputes; that poor women were accused exclusively of infanticide; that middle-class daughters were more often the victims of rape or seduction (or more to the point, that their abuse counted in the eyes of the courts). Des Essarts' class and gender bias reveals his prejudice that virtue could best be found amongst the middling sectors of society who were neither corrupted by wealth nor poverty and that women were more likely than their male counterparts to possess virtue regardless from which class they came.

The *Causes célèbres* thus perpetuated the illusion of ideological neutrality by focusing on "ordinary" people. At the same time, defense strategies featured therein advanced an Enlightenment critique of the Old Regime that was anything but politically neutral. As Bell writes of lawyers' memoirs generally: "While the majority of Parisian lawyers continued to go about routine business, the elite of the profession concerned themselves with what can only be called politics. Every case they fought had two audiences, the judges and 'public opinion,' and two purposes, the vindication of their clients and the implementation of enlightened reform."[20] Even some "routine business," the representation of clients embroiled in a domestic disturbance, was political as well, in that it advanced Enlightenment reform and challenged traditional forms of authority.

The attack on the tyrannical exercise of paternal power, for example, ubiquitous in the *Causes célèbres,* could scarcely be read as apolitical in the 1780s.[21] In case after case, lawyers attempted to persuade magistrates to limit paternal authority not just for the good of sons and daughters, but even more for the greater good of society. These lawyers did not always win their cases, but Des Essarts presented their rhetoric in such a way that readers sympathized with the cause of the victimized child or abused wife, for example, whose only crime was to fall in love with the wrong person, thus destroying the family's matrimonial strategy. Indeed, the *Causes célèbres* is important precisely because it reveals that norms for behavior could emanate from places other than courts' verdicts, that they stemmed more directly from the idealized roles introduced to readers of "causes célèbres" by lawyers whose rhetorical powers were tantamount to legislation itself. Darline Levy concludes that "Such a lawyer was not only an advocate; he was a de facto legislator. He convicted in spite of established law, even in blatant defiance of it. The judges whom he exhorted to disregard written law would be doing so as executors of his, the orator's, legislation, or as legislators themselves, making the advocate's word their law."[22] This is precisely the trajectory described by Maza that led to the Terror.

The ascendancy of trial literature in particular is underscored by this description of French society in which lawyers arguing cases on the eve of the French Revolution infused their presentation with politically loaded rhetoric, deliberately departing from a dry presentation of the "facts." This legal "style" reaches a deadly, but logical conclusion in the Terrorist prejudice against cold and "impartial reason." According to Carol Blum, "The very expression 'judicial impartiality' implies a set of cold, intellectualized, procedure-ridden attitudes which the republic of virtue wished to replace with a more emotionally immediate and hence morally superior method of justice."[23] Moreover, the evolution in lawyers' discourse testifies to more than the politicization of domestic court cases; it also reveals the extent to which sentimental and melodramatic narrative had pervaded French written and aural culture. And it is no accident that politicization and sentimentalization happen concurrently. As melodrama is the most democratic of all literary genres, it provided an appropriate language for proto-revolutionary calls for liberty, equality, and fraternity.

Leaving aside the trajectory towards Terror, it is clear that even during the Old Regime, court cases generate complex historical documents, rendering factual information opaque, infused as they are with lawyers' rhetoric, targeted to appeal to sentiment. Alain Lottin describes the difficulties: "[Lawyers'] influence can intervene at every level, not only in the presentation of the facts, in the argumentation, in the summations, but also, insidiously, in the very content of the disagreement. They can incite plaintiffs or defendants to invoke false motives and facts which they didn't think of, or push them, on the contrary, to conceal the truth."[24]

The *Causes célèbres* is at least one more step removed from historical fact than Lottin's court cases, especially in that Des Essarts was by no means rigorous or regular about citing his sources. More often than not, Des Essarts failed to use quotation marks, even after noting that a given section was in the words of one of the parties. Mostly he paraphrased, but interjected his own voice so often that it is clear he did not limit himself to the actual lawyers' briefs. Occasionally he took cases from other sources, "hearsay," or the "public papers," in which case he would offer a disclaimer at the outset: "We do not guarantee the accuracy of the things we are about to report. We have taken them from the public papers. We do not know if the anecdote is true, but it will certainly interest our readers."[25] Thus he was clearly concerned with authenticity; he eagerly linked his own voice with those of some of the lawyers, assuming their posture as arbiters of truth, but shunned associating himself with the less reputable popular press. In light of these obstacles to identifying precise voices, I will emphasize Des Essarts' omnipresence as narrator throughout the *Causes célèbres.*

Yet, perhaps the point is moot. Perhaps Des Essarts' rhetoric, if not his agenda, and that of a given lawyer arguing a *cause célèbre* are one and the same. Comparisons of Des Essarts' accounts with extant lawyers' dossiers reveal almost no departure from the lawyers' texts on the part of Des Essarts.[26] Indeed, lawyers also marketed their briefs for a mass audience. These memoirs were uncensored pamphlets ranging from five to two hundred pages in length, written by lawyers on their clients' behalf as "autobiographical" accounts of the case, accompanied by the supporting documentation contained in lawyers' dossiers. Maurice Daumas describes them: "Drafted by the lawyer on the instructions of his client, the memoir was destined for the court, but often dispersed to the public sometimes by the dozen."[27] But Maza calculates that "in the 1770s press runs [of lawyers' dossiers] of 3000 to 6000 were usual in big court cases, and by the time of the Sanois case, printings of 10,000 or more were not uncommon."[28]

Emotionally and politically charged discourse is found equally in Des Essarts and in the briefs themselves. According to Lottin, legal discourse itself rendered identifiable historical facts ever more obscure as the eighteenth century progressed, precisely because of the hyperbolic and emotional rhetorical style prevalent in lawyers' briefs. Moreover, lawyers' memoirs were not censored. Thus, not only in the *Causes célèbres,* but also in their own briefs, lawyers used cases as opportunities to express political opinions unmolested.

In eighteenth-century France, courts of law were the primary theaters of contestation in which nothing less than evolving definitions of citizenship were at stake. Staged as they were in court, the *Causes célèbres* must have had special appeal in a society which, according to David Bell, "from the princely houses to the humblest villages, seemed in a permanent state of litigation."[29] Details emerging from court cases provided popular subject matter, not just for the reading public who purchased "memoires judiciaires" or *causes célèbres,* but also for the nonreading public who learned of courtroom dramas in a variety of ways, including popular songs. Lenard Berlan-stein cites examples in his monograph on Toulousan barristers. "After the successful defense of a widow, an orphan or a pauper, the barrister's humanitarian concern might be celebrated in verse, and when he handled a case involving socially prominent people, he could become the center of public attention."[30]

Perhaps this was one of Des Essarts' motivations. Born in 1744 in Coutances, Des Essarts moved to Paris and became a lawyer.[31] While performing his functions for the "cour de cassation," he became an author, editor, and member of several academies. Among his most famous compilations is the *Dictionnaire universelle de police,* another encyclopedic enterprise, published in Paris between 1786–89. He wrote plays with titles such as *Emile et Sophie,* situating him squarely in the Rousseauian intersection of sensibility and republicanism, making him also a disciple of virtue. Throughout the Revolution, he continued compiling collections of literature and *causes célèbres* until his death in 1810. In 1797 he published *La vie et les crimes de Robespierre et de ses principaux complices, avec le détail des circonstances qui ont accompagné leur supplice.* Calling Robespierre's coterie a "hord of cannibals," Des Essarts revealed his Girondist leanings, including sympathetic accounts of the trials of Manon Roland and Charlotte Corday in his *Procès fameux jugés depuis la Révolution.*[32]

Thus the successful lawyer and the aspiring dramatist used serialized court cases to achieve fame. Apparently, depictions of court cases were in vogue. Des Essarts attributes this to everyone's insatiable desire to know the human heart: "This interest is so potent; it captivates the public's attention with so much force that the most seductive art (that of our theaters) takes the majority of its subjects from the types of stories that we report."[33]

Because of their adaptability to song and performance art, the cases of the *Causes célèbres* presented all members of French society—literate or not—with the widest array of gendered representations. Taken together, the *causes célèbres*—in whatever version one encountered them—of prerevolutionary France were both cause and consequence of a cultural revolution which anticipated the eruption in politics in 1789. Maza concludes that the "causes célèbres of the prerevolutionary decades not only reflected this [protracted cultural revolution covering roughly the second half of the eighteenth century], but contributed crucially to it."[34] In *Private Lives and Public Affairs,* she describes how the big political trials of the period, including the "Diamond Necklace" and Kornmann Affairs, facilitated this cultural revolution. Des Essarts, ignored such conspicuous and overtly political cases, a fact which Maza finds "curious."[35] She therefore chooses to omit his *Causes célèbres* from her study. Yet, these cases are only apparently apolitical; in this resides their potency. At the intersection of representation and reality, they uniquely attest to the ways in which discourses of virtue translated into everyday life.

In spite of the tragic tale of love and death which opened this chapter, most *causes célèbres* have "happier" endings. Interventions by magistrates, persuaded by the emotional rhetoric of lawyers, mitigate the sufferings of the virtuous in most of these tales, despite, in some cases, the mistaken verdicts of public opinion. Because M—— took his spouse's life, any opportunity for enlightened intervention was foreclosed. Obtaining a separation under the Old Regime, or better yet a divorce under the new, could have enabled M——to meet a less disastrous end.

This brief glance at an otherwise exemplary *causes célèbre* enabled a consideration of the editorial strategies behind this compilation and a glimpse of the appeal that such tearjerkers exercised upon an increasingly large and diverse audience of readers, individuals who collectively constituted a literary public sphere. The rapidly developing political culture of the late eighteenth century provided the context and furnished men of law and letters alike with opportunities to advocate an agenda which can be called "prerevolutionary." The terms honor and virtue recur throughout the *Causes célèbres* and the contestation over their meaning and relation fuels an explosive discussion, one of the outcomes of which is the Republic of Virtue.

Cognizant of Des Essarts' editorial strategies, of the wide appeal of the *Causes célèbres,* and of the cultural revolution underway in the last decades of the eighteenth century, it is appropriate to begin an explication of several exemplary cases.

2
Domestic Magistracy: Seductions

> How grand, how respectable is the authority of fathers over their children, above all in matters of marriage; it should however be contained within limits. This domestic magistracy, as holy as it is, has its limits relative to the interests of society. . . . fathers cannot serve themselves at all times and on all occasions. . . . We know that nature and law have made, within families, as many sovereigns as there are fathers; but we want to purify the use of their authority, to mitigate its exercise by the just and ingenious means that our laws have adopted.[1]

So argued Barère de Vieuzac before the Parlement of Toulouse in 1784. Castigating an aristocratic father for breaking up his son's marriage, Barère urged the magistrates to issue a judgement favorable to the abandoned spouse, Catherine Noailles, by calling for appropriate strictures against domestic tyranny.

Calls for the limitation of paternal authority, proliferating in the 1780s, can be read as thinly veiled attacks on royal absolutism. Read more literally, they imply that new roles for men and women were promulgated as part of a discourse on citizenship which mandated a submission of personal "interest" to the "interests of society," or what would later be called the "general will." Moreover, it was often women like Catherine Noailles who called for and eventually benefitted from the limitations placed on male behavior by anti-absolutist and anti-aristocratic men.

Afar from static structure, revisions of patriarchy occur whenever social or political structures are reevaluated. For example, at the end of the seventeenth century in Britain which had undergone a period of revolution, "contract theorists, Locke notably, . . . cast doubt on the origin and the extent of paternal power: it is the case where the liberty of the individual can and should be opposed to the power of the father, whose golden age is henceforth in decline."[2] Thus resulted in the eighteenth century an "enlightenment paternity," which is compatible with the advent of the free citizen across Europe. Thus resulted a spate of verdicts in which sons and daughters enjoyed favorable hearings in the cases they brought to court.[3]

Lynn Hunt explained in *The Family Romance of the French Revolution* that the appearance of the good father was a signal that his erasure was imminent. For Hunt, Freud's theory of the family romance invites new readings of the French Revolution because "the most obvious material at hand for thinking politically was the family, not the family as some kind of modal social experience, but the family as an imaginative construct of power relations."[4] Because Old Regime critics of the monarchy were reticent about attacking the king personally, lawyers symbolically challenged him as they litigated against self-interested fathers in the 1770s and 80s. Attacks on fathers are abundant in the *Causes célèbres* as their power threatened civil society, especially when their self interests were incompatible with the greater good. With the outbreak of revolution, "family romances"—stories in which the excesses of male authority are challenged by family members, brought to the attention of the legal system, and then mitigated—functioned as blueprints for a new world order. The rhetoric and imagery of prerevolutionary legal and melodramatic discourse fostered the evolution of the king from absolutist tyrant into domesticated good father and then in turn anticipated his erasure, as Hunt contends.

The *Causes célèbres*, as both fact and fiction, news and fantasy, provide an unique point of entry into the "collective unconscious/political imagination"—to use Hunt's words—of prerevolutionary France. Underpinning all three cases of seduction described below are conflicts between traditional and enlightened, aristocratic and bourgeois, and male and female conceptions of honor. In all three the critique of traditional forms of authority is accompanied by an implicit definition of republican citizenship which revolved around the possession and manifestation of virtue.

Catherine Noailles was born on August 4, 1756, the daughter of a prominent member of Beaucaire's bourgeoisie: her father was a man of commerce, a merchant sea captain. Barère emphasized this to the magistrates: Noailles was not to be found in "the class of fishermen, but in that of merchants; . . . . in a useful class, in an honest station which calls forth abundance and augments national industry."[5] Throughout the case, told alternately by Barère and omnipresent narrator Des Essarts, the virtues of the bourgeoisie stand out in sharp contrast to the corrupt blue-blooded aristocracy with whom their lives intertwine.

At 16, Catherine made the acquaintance of François-Joseph de Rois, youngest son of Beaucaire's oldest and most blue-blooded family; his father held the prestigious title of chevalier de Saint-Louis. Indeed this family's name was so illustrious that lawyers' memoirs and other accounts of the case referred to François as "chevalier de ___," the litigant's family clearly preferring anonymity to scandal. But Des Essarts only sometimes left the litigants in his stories anonymous. When protecting anonymity he claimed to possess more integrity than the editors of other "public papers." But he sometimes "slipped," naming litigants who wished to remain anonymous, as if by accident, especially if letters were quoted, for in the letters names were usually indicated. His "slips" usually occurred in cases involving aristocrats such as de Rois. Arbiter of public opinion, Des Essarts knew how to exact his own vengeance against the non-virtuous. He also doubtless knew that high-level scandal sold. In this account, he cited letters with signatures intact.

And plenty of letters there were. Slightly younger than Catherine, born on May 12, 1757, François fell in love with her. Wary of the dangers of this flirtation between this modest girl of the bourgeoisie and a hot-blooded, blue-blooded, young aristocrat, Catherine's father sent her to a relative in Toulouse for a year, hoping to derail this dangerous liaison.[6]

François wrote to Catherine, pledging his love and swearing it meant more to him than his family's obsession with misalliance or derogation through marriage to a commoner. People in love, he insisted, should be able to tear asunder distinctions of social class. He wanted to marry her to prove they could overcome "the distance that society's prejudices have put between them."[7] Indeed, in his letters he revealed a radical egalitarianism, insisting that "All men are equal. Nobility should be granted only on the basis of personal merit; wealth comes from chance. One ought to designate as 'noble' the man most worthy of the name. . . . Probity, humanity, greatness of soul, generosity. These are the charms for me."[8] The acquisition of titles, privileges, and fortune was mere accident, he contended, having nothing to do with a person's real worth. Honor should be based on behavior. Thus flaunting his scorn for his pretentious noble background, he swore he would marry her no matter what. He even signed one letter in blood, spilling that substance which perpetuated distinctions between them in the first place, making a sacrificial offering to his beloved whose blood could never be as precious, as "blue."

Upon Catherine's return to Beaucaire, the two continued their liaison in spite of the opposition of both of their fathers. Servants in both households arranged secret meetings and delivered forbidden love letters. Often in these letters he referred to her as his wife: "Yes, miss, I regard you as that which I hold dearest in all the world, as my best friend, indeed as my wife."[9] In his version of the family romance, virtuous and honorable lovers make companionate marriages, marriages which are based solely on promises and good faith, not on law or custom or "prejudice" or some outmoded principle of honor.

Their love affair endured thus for nine years, and when Catherine reached the age of majority, 25, François determined to marry her.[10] A servant had procured for him a key to her room, and on March 4, 1781, he slipped in unnoticed, and, carriage waiting, led her away in the middle of the night. They set off for neighboring Montfavet where they lodged with an "honest citizen" and there he presented her with a marriage promise, allegedly signed by his father.

Shocked to discover his daughter's disappearance, Noailles' father pressed charges of "rape by seduction" against de Rois on April 24. Gaining intelligence of this legal action against him (again through servants), François begged the parish priest to intervene, urging that their clandestine marriage be celebrated as soon as possible. This indulgent priest, moved by the plight of these star-crossed lovers, performed the marriage on September 15, the earliest possible date allowed by law, six months after they had taken up legal residence in Montfavet. Already in his 70s, Catherine's father had little choice at this point but to accept his daughter's marriage, recognizing that it was the only way to avoid the scandal of a trial and save her honor, for a seduced woman was a dishonored woman in the eyes of the public. He therefore dropped charges. In the meantime, the de Rois family initially tolerated François' marriage to a commoner because he was not their principal heir.

Shortly thereafter, the eldest de Rois, "the hope of the lineage" and heir to the family titles, died. Eager to reconcile with his family, François brought his bride to meet them in the winter of 1782. His sister received her warmly, but recommended that he seek a rapprochement with the patriarchs of the family, namely his father and uncle, first. Alone. Catherine remained with his sister while he approached his parents. His family, led by his apparently cruel uncle, decided to end their tolerance of the marriage and declared they would have it annulled. The uncle kidnapped François, confining him to his deceased brother's rooms by means of a "lettre de cachet."

"Lettres de cachet" were used by noble families to prevent scandal, illustrating the degree to which they too were preoccupied with maintaining a reputation for honor. Arlette Farge describes them: "Arrest without attracting attention, preventing scandal, burying the crime and the criminal, this a mere royal gesture, the very essence of the 'lettre de cachet.'"[11] Writing of another case, Des Essarts found this to be just in principle, even if he resented its use by the status-conscious aristocracy: "Each family has the right to exercise, over each one of its members, this type of correctional justice, and to prevent the dishonor of one's conduct or follies from reflecting back on it."[12] De Rois' father would have thought himself vindicated by these words because a young noble's sexual misbehavior could apparently ruin his family. Des Essarts continued: "It is no doubt a misfortune for families that their honor depends on the behavior of a young fool who knows no other rule than his passion. . . ."[13] An excess of passion leads to ruin, and its publicity will compel the public to dishonor the fool and his family, no matter how blue-blooded. Thus, fooling the public and avoiding a *causes célèbre* required concealing transgression. Such honorable dissimulation is why revolutionaries would come to prefer transparent virtue.

De Rois' attempts to correspond with Catherine were for the most part thwarted by his determined uncle, and after March she heard nothing more from him until a year later when she learned he had married someone else in Marseilles. There the narrative resumes. Catherine had been living with her parents as was appropriate for an abandoned woman at the time. Horrified at this betrayal, and at the imminent dishonor which would befall Catherine and her family, her father filed complaint on May 23, 1783. A bitter "cause célèbre" ensued in which parents on both sides debated the legitimacy of the original marriage, but disagreed about who was to blame, each lawyer arguing that his client was the victim of a vile seducer.

With the assistance of their lawyer, de Rocques, the de Rois family set out to prove that none of the procedures necessary for a valid marriage were followed by the young couple, and that therefore there had never been a marriage between them: Noailles was merely his concubine. Indeed, in their opinion, she herself was guilty of rape by seduction. After all, she was older than their unwitting son, and de Rocques protested that "rape by seduction admits no distinction by sex."[14] However, this role reversal also threatened the de Rois family honor in its masculine content, since according to this reasoning, an enterprising bourgeois woman controlled a powerful man.

Even though Catherine based her case on her desire to fulfill her appropriate role in society, the de Rois family obtained favorable judgments annulling the marriage at Arles in May and June of 1783. The Noailles family appealed the lower court's decision to the supreme court of the region, the parlement of Toulouse.

Barère de Vieuzac defended Catherine and her family, arguing that the chevalier—François' newly gained title—was at least guilty of seduction and more likely bigamy. Barère did not deny that the marriage to Noailles lacked the proper legal underpinnings, but he insisted that some marriages must still be accepted as legitimate: "I know, sirs, that the validity of marriages demands the concourse of religion and civil law, but when nature, religion, and probity have already formed a union, can family interests, the speculations of fortune and vanity, break it?"[15] There is, then, more to a marriage than following prescribed rites. Because the couple had lived conjugally, because they consummated their union, and most importantly, because the public recognized them as spouses, they were married—in the eyes of nature, religion, and society. It was only the selfish interests of a noble family who sought to throw suspicion upon the legitimacy of the marriage.

Though Des Essarts believed that distinctions in society must be maintained, he praised the English disregard of constraints on choice in marriage partner in his account of a case involving an English couple. In England, a country lauded by "philosophes" for its more reasonable and enlightened approach to family and state, the concept "misalliance" is so unknown that there is not even a word for it: "In England, one repulses with the greatest force, as a national danger, these conventions so precious among us regarding marriages, [while in France] the sole word 'mésalliance' is a battle cry, which sets in motion—by rumor—families, societies, cities, and entire provinces."[16] Though marriages between nobles and bourgeois had taken place for centuries, their increasing frequency apparently alarmed families like de Rois who wanted to close ranks; Des Essarts' concern about this closing of ranks demonstrates its prevalence by the 1780s.

Barère continued the tirade against "misalliance": "With this word misalliance they have hoped to elevate the nobility. Is there among gentlemen, among other citizens, is there one single man who, after having seduced a young woman, after having run off with her, after having made reparations by marriage, can then retract his promises, falsify his words, relegate his victim into the lowest class of citizens?"[17] By abandoning his wife, marrying another, then insinuating that his legal wife was merely a concubine, de Rois, giving into the demands of his father and uncle, created out of the woman he once loved the most lamentable victim, a woman who may still be a citizen but who has sunk to the lowest possible level. A woman who was seduced and abandoned would no longer be able to fulfil her principal obligation to the state: to rear legitimate and upright citizens for the nation. Thus by abandoning Catherine, François not only dishonored her, but ruined her forever.

By dramatizing her tragedy, and by trivializing, indeed, demonizing, the nobility's concerns, Barère believed he could move the court to rule in her favor. He appealed to their abhorrence of the wasted, useless woman, saying, "it is better that there exist in society a legitimate wife than a deceived woman, a husband, even unfaithful, than an unpunished seducer."[18] If their marriage was indeed a model for the social contract, then his violation of it constituted a crime against the state as well. In becoming her husband, he accepted certain responsibilities, towards her and towards the state. Elsewhere, Des Essarts explained: "When a man contracts a marriage, he forms a tacit contract with society which receives new citizens from him. A celibate man looks only after himself whereas a father of a family looks after the state. . . . . His children belong to the state; his spouse is under the surveillance of public decency; he must not compromise the fate of the latter, nor the honor of the former."[19]

The celibate man, like the libertine, is therefore self-interested, whereas a republican father is devoted to the public good, recognizing that children belong not to their biological fathers but to the nation.[20] Equally corrupt is the self-interested father, and in this case seducer/husband. Any man who neglects his family neglects the state. By abandoning Catherine, de Rois shirked his responsibilities to the state. He rejected his own citizenship in the process of destroying hers.

Besides, he continued, the marriage was not really that much of a "misalliance"; Catherine was, after all, not the daughter of a peasant or a laborer. Had she been, we may have seen the limits of Barère's egalitarianism.[21] But the Noailles family belonged to that class of citizens most worthy of the state's esteem. Rather than seeing marriage to members of this class as a source of dishonor, the nobility would do well to augment its own wealth and stature, as well as the state's, by aligning itself to this most useful and honest class, the bourgeoisie. Of course such alliances had existed for centuries; thus Barère's plea is a rhetorical device meant to reveal the absurdity of the de Rois' rhetorical device that revolved around an anachronistic notion of honor.

Barère was unwilling to allow the nobility to abuse other people's honor only to claim they must protect their own. He redefined honor, linking it very specifically to appropriate behavior: "Ah! honor, real honor is not always in the opulence of a mere name, nor in brilliantly made marriages; honor is in keeping promises, and in respecting someone's faith."[22] And again: "Real honor is to be just, to repair the damages one has done; to keep one's word, to respect one's oaths; and to not do wrong out of vanity."[23] To be faithful, true, honest, and just—in that behavior can be found the source of honor, pure and simple. Anyone can keep a promise, unless motivated by greed and vanity, as were most nobles. Extrapolating, the democratization of standards of worth applied more readily to classes other than the nobility. With austere civic standards of behavior serving as the prerequisite for honor ("a father of a family looks after the state . . ."), the frivolous, "self-interested" nobility would have the greatest difficulty obtaining it; their existence would become incompatible with a society based upon a republican notion of honor.

Barère believed that the young de Rois was torn between two conflicting notions of honor, that espoused by his father and uncle, and that by his wife: that of the traditional male aristocrat and that of the virtuous bourgeois female. Noailles' honor was "ravished" from her by an aristocrat who refused to regard her as his wife on the basis of maintaining the biological integrity of his class—the source of aristocratic honor. Even de Rois' lawyer makes this conflict between competing notions of honor more explicit by deliberately juxtaposing them. He chided Catherine: "Demoiselle Noailles should detest her victory if it costs her 'husband' his honor," i.e., his good name.[24] Noailles answered in turn that the man she married had now chosen wealth over faith, obedience over honor, father over wife. Through Barère she pleaded: "Perfidious and blind chevalier, from whom I have received a hand in marriage when you were poor, and who throws me out of your house when you have become rich, listen to my defense. . . . [c]onjugal faith, true honor" should determine the chevalier to return to his wife and accept disinheritance.[25] He should accept his father's chastisement, realizing that real honor lies not in blindly obeying a corrupt father, but in being faithful.

Thus, the conflict between these two notions of honor has a class, but also a gender component; Catherine will lose her honor as a woman if the chevalier guards his as an aristocrat. In other words, real honor like real virtue is a matter of character, behavior, not blood. Real honor arises from the internalization of civil society's norms, from its definition of virtue, not from the will of a tyrannical and self-interested father.

According to this thinking, then, de Rois is obliged by his own conscience to disobey his father. Emphasizing public over selfish interest, lawyers argued that the interested father had no claim to legitimate authority and could therefore be disobeyed with impunity: resentment on the part of the oppressed always leads to a diminution of the power of the oppressor. Writ large, however, such admonitions to disobedience might even lead to revolution. Though an eventual revolutionary himself, Des Essarts was keenly aware of this possibility and offered this prescient observation in 1786:

> You see, sirs, how we begin to be astonished that a father exercises the right that the law has given him to avenge his betrayed honor, his scorned authority. We will finish by refusing him this right; from the impossibility of punishing children will spring contempt for fathers, insubordination, revolt. And in the middle of this universal anarchy, what resource will be left for the law when the severity of punishment becomes an excuse for impunity?[26]

Des Essarts was alarmed that disrespect for law would result from the collapse of patriarchal authority, from "contempt for fathers." He saw that laws are an expression of patriarchy—an embodiment of the father, according to Freud's theory of the "family romance"—and that waning respect for the father could lead to lawlessness or "universal anarchy." Yet he would not say that a father's authority, nor the king's, should be absolute. How to resolve this dilemma? How to temper patriarchy without undermining it? According to Hunt, the struggle over such questions provides a constant narrative of the revolution. "The revolutionaries wanted liberty and equality to rule in the family just as they ruled in the state, though just what was meant by liberty and equality in the context of the family remained subject to continual redefinition. Revolutionary legislators were clearest about what they opposed: tyrannical power within the family."[27]

Barère would become one such legislator unambiguous in his opposition to tyranny in the public or private spheres. And in his defense of Catherine Noailles he was unambiguous in his depiction of her father-in-law as a self-interested tyrant. He argued that a father's authority is not the final tribunal, and that it must be restrained by the law to keep fathers from advancing their own selfish interests at the expense of those of society, or even those of sons: "Paternal authority is upheld by the tribunal for the benefit of the son and not for the avarice of parents."[28]

Yet in the 1780s, revolution could have been avoided. Perhaps intermediaries could intercede on the son's (or daughter's) behalf. This is precisely the role of the law in as much as figurative fathers, magistrates, could be counted on to promote "public" interest, immune as they were to personal interest. Again, Des Essarts summed it up best when commenting on that case involving the English couple in which he assured the female litigant, "You will find a father in the heart of each magistrate." "As for the magistrates, they know no other sentiments than those that purify an always impartial reason: they are familiar with legislative secrets, and they know better than anyone that the interest of one individual should not suppress the general interest of society."[29] "Impartial Reason" was, therefore, a force superior to the will of fathers or even to the mandates of aristocratic tradition. "Impartial Reason," channeled through magistrates who are its mouthpiece, would sustain the "general interest of society" by limiting any one individual's power and by assuring that individual interests are held in check. "Impartial Reason," contextualized here as the ultimate source of authority, portends the revolutionary festivals and cults organized in its name so central to the Republic of Virtue. Barère goes further and equates Reason with the true fount of all authority, the "Supreme Being," evoked here to delimit even further a father's claims: "A spouse married by the tribunal of honor, engaged before the Supreme Being, should he obey the cupidity of his family or the voice of his conscience?"[30] De Rois eloped with a woman he wanted to marry; they consecrated their union before the tribunal of honor, where, loyal to their hearts they made promises they swore they would keep, and before a force even greater than religion with its petty prescriptions, nothing less than the Supreme Being. How can the law suppose that there is any union more valid than that? How can a father's greed be esteemed a superior cause?

Both the worship of Reason and the Cult of the Supreme Being were anticipated in Barère's rhetoric, for on religious matters, he was a man of the Enlightenment *par excellence*, rejecting the God of the popes, placing in its stead a rational, objective, and just being, a god made after the image of the Enlightened man himself, who understood Christianity's true meaning to be radical egalitarianism: "The holiness of Christianity has finally banished every difference that fortune puts between men; grace knows no distinctions between people."[31] If social class is ultimately meaningless, then the commission of injustices in its name must be condemned now, by earthly judges, rather than deferring until the last judgement. Rather than deferring until the Revolution when radicals attempted to temper social distinctions, issuing rhetorical appeals such as this.

Ironically, the young de Rois seduced Noailles with similar rhetoric, urging her to believe that differences between people were artificial, erected by those members of society obsessed with antiquated definitions of honor. The court took de Rois' romantic words seriously, ruling that his nobility, and the honor he was purporting to protect, did not excuse his inappropriate behavior. He was a "ravisseur" and owed to his victim the most that could be offered her: financial retribution.

The parlement of Toulouse ruled in her favor on March 29, 1784. A settlement of 20,000 livres was granted on June 1, significantly less than the 80,000 demanded. But is a monetary payment the appropriate way to restore a woman's lost honor? Maurice Daumas points out the paradox of using money as a means of compensation: "But how to measure the affront without mentioning money and how to claim monetary compensation without being accused of forgetting honor?"[32] Forced into litigation by a bourgeois family, the de Rois had no choice but to settle matters this way. Forced to litigate by a bourgeois family, the court mandated a cash settlement to the wronged woman. But it would go no further. Magistrates did not respect the victim's insistence, voiced by Barère, that the marriage was legitimate, an acknowledgment which would thereby force the chevalier to return to his wife. He was a "ravisseur" and not a bigamist; the court wanted it both ways. It punished the criminal, but refused to save the victim. Because the marriage between de Rois and Noailles lacked de Rois' father's consent, the court declared it invalid, still privileging legality over promises of love, consummation, conjugal cohabitation, and public opinion, still maintaining the rule of fathers.

But not for long. In the final analysis, the court's ruling proves that it was sensitive to Barère's line of argumentation: the state would set limits on paternal authority; the state would penalize abusers of women; the state would subject the nobility to the same standards of behavior as the bourgeoisie. Barère would go on to win many more cases, advancing each time an agenda informed by Enlightenment precepts and setting the stage for the Republic of Virtue. For example, in marriage negotiations, Barère urged community of goods because "In the era of liberty, there should remain no form of despotism."[33] Even a husband's despotism would be tempered, as we shall see in the next chapter.

And Barère was not the only one. Within ten years, the monarchy would be abolished, feudalism dismantled, and divorce legalized, largely due to the efforts of lawyers such as he, and due to publications such as the *Causes célèbres* which served to vindicate those who challenged abuses of established authority even when the courts themselves did not. Furthermore, as Maza points out, court cases "demonstrate[d] that the experiences of ordinary people were important enough to serve as a foundation for moral and legal norms."[34] Though some verdicts were ambiguous, in law as in morals the *Causes célèbres* set standards for men and women, for fathers who ought to curb their behavior for the benefit of civil society, for husbands who must recognize their obligations under the social contract, and for wives and daughters whose good behavior, whose pure and virtuous reputations, were necessary to the performance of their civic duties.

Fortunately for Catherine, her liaison with de Rois did not result in pregnancy. Illegitimacy complicates the next case in which another noble seduces a social inferior. The resulting offspring exacerbates the potential for dishonor that both sides face.

> "M. Marsanges," she said one day while seated at his feet, "it is time to save the honor that I am about to lose, and to assure our child the status you have destined for it."
>
> "I cannot satisfy you," he responded coldly, "particular considerations oppose it."
>
> "Eh! what are, sir, these considerations? Are they stronger than the promises and oaths you have made to me? Can they not be countered by honor, by virtue, and by religion?"
>
> "You are not noble, and, in marrying you, I would marry beneath myself."
>
> "You have really dishonored me forever, and you cannot return the honor that you have ravished from me because I am not noble!"[35]

Here the abandoned woman, Thérèse Martin, used the word honor four times, which suggests that different kinds of honor were at stake. Her seducer had two separate opportunities to ravish her honor: the first being the seduction itself, the second being the failure to redeem her reputation publicly by marrying her. This failure was not only an offense to her honor, but to a larger transcendent honor, the one that mandated respect for public order. Thus, the second time she uttered the word was in an effort to persuade Marsanges to make amends: "honor," like "virtue" and "religion," was in this instance an independent force which carried enough authority to inform a person's actions, even those of the aristocrat who was claiming the primacy of other motivating forces, like the honor of his name and the social class which stood behind him.

Martin's father was a wholesaler of produce in Fontainebleau. After his premature death, her mother married a groundskeeper at a royal estate in 1766 when Thérèse was 10 years old. Thus we have here an absent father, with a stepfather serving as the family patriarch. In charge of the estate was Bernard Marsanges, a wealthy single aristocrat. For the next eight years Marsanges solicited the affection of Martin and her parents, convincing all that he intended to marry her. And when Thérèse herself questioned this man's behavior, her parents, blinded by their own ambition, assured her of his sincerity. On October 15, 1774, Marsanges ordered Thérèse's parents to perform obligatory functions at the estate, thus insuring that no one but Thérèse would be at home. The literal absence of the father is foundational to this drama. This abuse of power was followed by still others. Ignoring a servant's insistence that he refrain from entering Martin's room, he went to her, locking the door behind him. Des Essarts tells us a "criminal love" ensued.

This "love" left Martin pregnant. She demanded that Marsanges fulfill his promise to marry her. He ignored the demands, her reasoning, her tears—insisting that he would do himself and his class an injustice by marrying a commoner. Taking up the cause, her stepfather also urged Marsanges to remember his promises. Again to no avail. Justice would have to intervene on her behalf.

Hoping to force Marsanges' hand by making public his crime, Martin's stepfather registered a charge of rape by seduction against Marsanges, at which time Marsanges offered a sum of money in remuneration. His offer was conditional, however: the newly born son would have to be placed in an orphanage, and the father's name stricken from the birth record. Outraged at this suggestion, Martin's stepfather brought Marsanges before the court where Marsanges claimed that his paternity could never be proved, but that, out of generosity, he would see to the child's upbringing. His denial of paternity dealt another blow to Thérèse's honor by publicly calling her virtue into question. Martin sued for an annual pension of 1000 livres for the rearing of the child and for 12,000 livres in damages. The court ruled that Martin could raise the child for seven years, receiving an annual pension from Marsanges of 300 livres. After seven years the child would pass into the care of Marsanges. The award of damages was reduced to 6000 livres.

Though the court's verdict did not satisfy the monetary demands of the Martin family, it did vindicate their charges, especially when it mandated that the child would be cared for by Marsanges at age seven, acknowledging him guilty of seduction and of fathering the child. Des Essarts applauded the verdict. He describes Marsanges' plan as though it were a military operation, thus revealing the stereotype of the bellicose and rapacious aristocrat. For example, he described Martin as "the unfortunate one whom he wanted to make his prey," and told us Marsanges' intentions accordingly: "He pretended to respect the one he wanted to dishonor, to adore the one he wanted to profane. He had the power to make her his slave in order to become a cruel tyrant."[36] Marsanges was thus a master of deception, bent on the destruction of his "prey." Finally, describing the moment when Marsanges' plan would be brought to fruition, Des Essarts reported: "He judged that his victim was ready and that it was time to consummate the sacrifice."[37] And, upon finding Martin alone, we are told that he ignored her protestations: "Marsanges heard nothing; he entered, closed the door, and snatched the sacrifice that he had prepared for so long."[38] Was it rape?

The negative stereotypes of the aristocracy evoked by Des Essarts stand out in sharp contrast to the sympathetic yet cliché-ridden language he used when discussing Martin, a virtuous and innocent victim of her parents' ambition and a predatory aristocrat. Des Essarts depicted her plight in these terms: "Demoiselle Martin realized all the horror of her situation: she saw her honor lost; she only saw her mother and stepfather as justly angered persecutors; and adding to her troubles, the sad destiny of the innocent victim who drew from her womb the germ of life and of shame presented itself in her imagination."[39] Her child would forever be dishonored because of its shameful origins, just as she would be, despite the court's verdict.

Just as a lawyer's rhetoric would move the magistrates, his tear-jerking words moved readers to sympathize with the victim whose honor had been cruelly ravished from her, whose love for her unborn child, another innocent victim, only deepened her anguish.

The trope of the long-suffering natural mother, whose instinctive love for a child whose existence manifests her shame, is evoked repeatedly in the *Causes célèbres* to illustrate women's self-sacrifice, a defining feature of their innate virtue. Though Marsanges stole her honor, he could not damage her virtue, which remained her only consolation. At the same time, his actions proved his lack of virtue and dishonored him as well.

After abusing his noble privileges in order to seduce Martin (by ordering her parents away from the estate, thus leaving her alone), Marsanges evoked them when he explained his refusal to marry her, implying that such a marriage would be a source of dishonor for him. Moreover, by demanding that his name be purged from the infant's baptismal record, he acknowledged that his libertinage would dishonor him. According to Des Essarts, "he did not want the existence of any proof of his paternity because of the prejudice this would bring against his fortune and rank."[40] Apparently Marsanges knew that his actions, if publicized, would bring dishonor upon himself and his class. Like de Rois, he had to insure the biological integrity of his class as well as the reputation of his name. Here, too, it was not the action itself, but its publicity that led to a loss of honor; his reputation for inappropriate sexual behavior would have implications. Women victimized by men would no longer be the only ones convicted by the tribunal of public opinion. Because of Marsange's anxiety about the *publicity* of his transgression, one can infer that a more even application of standards of behavior to both sexes, of all classes, was beginning to become entrenched, as control over sexuality was extended even to the libertine of noble extraction.

Even though the verdicts in both cases considered thus far were not explicitly what the accused sought, the rulings did exact punishment even as they provided a public opportunity for women to decry the abuse they suffered while manifesting their virtue. Defending themselves against an increasingly hollow defense of aristocratic privilege, such women would find their vindication within a few years when those privileges were abolished. Beyond the aristocracy, however, other "domestic magistrates" found their power checked as well, as in the next case where paternal power itself is abused and then called into question; this man's authority did not stem from his class status, but rather from his role as father-of-the-family.

In Paris in 1774 M. Duel, a clothing cleaner, rented a third-floor apartment to M. Henry, located above his boutique. Duel's wife had recently died, and his oldest daughter, aged 15 at the time, had assumed her mother's role in managing the household and caring for the five other children. Henry was a poor errand boy and had difficulty paying the rent, yet he had befriended all of the children, and finally asked Duel for permission to marry the girl. Suspicious of Henry's morals, scornful of his low station in life, and aware that his daughter was in love, Duel refused and instead placed his daughter with the Ursulines at Argenteuil on March 4, 1774. He kept her there for three months, but upon her release, she and Henry resumed their love affair and she became pregnant. Her father returned her to the convent, but once her pregnancy became known, she was expelled.

Before her father retrieved her, she disappeared, allegedly with the help of sympathetic nuns. Thereafter she and her father played a game of cat and mouse, he locking her up in increasingly impenetrable places and she managing to escape, the most dramatic entailing escape from a room, dark and damp we are told, where she was fed only moldy black bread and water, secured with iron bars, grills, locks, and chains, and located 26 feet above the ground! And at the time of this escape she was eight months pregnant. Once again her father managed to find her even though she had changed identities and secured work in a stocking boutique. When he found her there, he allegedly beat her, in spite of her pregnancy. Neighbors intervened, and it was her father who received the worse thrashing this time.

Duel blamed Henry for facilitating his daughter's escapes, and indeed for leading her astray in the first place. On February 11, 1778, Duel filed charges of rape by seduction against Henry, who promptly interjected an appeal, claiming that he had not seduced the girl, that she had freely consented to everything, and that she escaped her father's imprisonment and blows on her own. On January 22, 1779, the court ruled that Henry and the girl must pay amends—three "livres" in bread to prisoners. Henry was condemned to pay the court costs and for the rearing of his son who had been born in the meantime. He was also allowed to retain custody of the child. The verdict then mandated confinement in a convent for Duel's daughter for an unspecified period of time, at her father's expense.

From the perspective of the verdict, the loser in this case is clearly the girl. Yet Des Essarts' rhetoric, as well as that of Henry's lawyer, Ader, was intended to pull readers' heartstrings, and evoke sympathy for this victim of an absolutist, tyrannical authority. Each lawyer offered competing definitions of fatherhood, the differences between them illustrating the tensions between traditional and prerevolutionary interpretations, between the two versions identified by Hunt—the absolutist father versus the good republican, civic-minded father.

According to Ader, Duel should have accepted the only real solution to this problem which was to allow the two to marry, thereby legitimizing his grandson and saving his daughter from public disgrace. Ader asked him: "What interest, what pleasure, what glory do you take in making these two children, who should be dear to you, perish in humiliation?"[41] As in the Noailles' case, the father allegedly had private "interests," interests which were by definition antithetical to the common good. Finding nothing of satisfaction in Duel's own rhetoric, Ader then told the court what a good father would say: "Henry and my daughter are not guilty because their intentions were pure; preserve the honor of the only person who can return my daughter to the esteem of men. Let them repair their mistakes at the foot of the altar."[42] Or as in another similar case where there were potentially illegitimate grandchildren, he might have recognized that "virtue has very potent rights; everything can be rectified."[43] Thus "virtue" in this view is once again touted to be an independent force with its own mandates and its own rights—and it must be obeyed. This distinguishes it from the more tentative "honor" which is conferred by the public, equated with the "esteem of men."

In Ader's rhetoric, it is not so much the girl's honor that is at stake, nor even that of her infant son, but rather it is Henry's. Ader urged Duel not to prosecute Henry, which would blemish his honor, because Duel needed Henry to rectify an otherwise hopeless situation. Ader insisted that Henry's intentions were always honorable, and this insistence itself proves that an accusation of seduction, of sexual misbehavior and transgression, could damage a man's honor. Ader even went so far as to insinuate that the girl was to blame for inflaming Henry's passions: "[D]emoiselle Duel's passion was intense; Henry would have been an ingrate for not responding."[44] But, really, he continued, neither is to blame: "Wasn't their inclination natural? They are about the same age; each one is attractive. . . . Isn't this in nature?"[45] Here, as in the Noailles' case, "Nature" is offered as a justification, above man-made laws, passionate attraction esteemed as the true basis for lasting and fruitful unions.

According to Ader, Duel should have pardoned and freed them, not merely in the interest of their happiness, but so that they might function as productive, respectable citizens. He should have remembered a maxim echoed in another case, involving similar issues: "Be sure of it: a father's honor and his daughter's are indivisible."[46] Both David Garrioch and Nicole Castan found this to be true in the communities they studied: "When family honour was at stake parents and children were inseparable." And "A golden rule dominated the members of these groups: the family and the patrimony first, then the individual. . . ."[47] These statements attest to the degree that representations like those in the *Causes célèbres* had meaning for audiences, in that the concerns of real people are reflected in the rhetoric of lawyers. The disagreement between the two litigants, then, was over the means by which family honor could best be restored once a seduction and illegitimate pregnancy transpired.

Therefore, to enhance his case, Ader goes even further by insisting that the well-being of society as a whole must come first—the interests of father and patrimony must be subordinate to those of the state. To allow his daughter to live in dishonor was to bring the same upon himself, according to Ader. In this case, everyone's honor was clearly at stake. Both Henry and Duel claimed to be defending the girl's honor, as well as their own. Only father magistrates, above narrow preoccupations with honor, could recognize virtue.

Throughout the *Causes célèbres*, magistrates are frequently appealed to as fathers in their own right, as well as fathers of every citizen, and indeed of the country: veritable patriarchs but in the sentimental, Enlightenment version described above. Desperately trying to move the court to be generous when considering the legitimacy of a Protestant's marriage, a lawyer appealed to the magistrate's own experience of paternity:

> You will recall the moment when you received, for the first time, in your arms trembling with joy, an infant who owes its life to you, when

> you smiled at it, covered with tears, when the smallest cries from this innocent creature took you by surprise and made you shudder all over. When, pressing against your breast mother and baby, carried away by mixed emotions, divided between compassion and joy, did you need then to recall the formalities of our laws to be constrained to tenderness? Did you doubt then that your engagement takes its force from nature?[48]

This language is reminiscent of Rousseau's description of the "Silver Age" described in *The Discourse on the Origins of Inequality*, complete with sentimental overtones, appeals to nature, and buttresses for patriarchy. At the same time, it locates legitimacy in the natural attraction and affection that develops between a virtuous man and woman. Magistrates, as fathers, were supposed to be able to identify with the cause of every father, but whether or not such figurative fathers should uphold laws or indulge sentiment was hotly contested. Appealing thus to their sentiments, a lawyer could hope to move their hearts to grant a favorable judgement, bypassing their adherence to the letter of the law. But even more to the point are the numerous cases in which magistrates were explicitly appealed to as public "fathers"; they were above the private interests of a "father of a family" and thereby better able to legislate for the common good. In a case where an illegitimate girl was accused of a crime, her lawyer assured her: "The more [defendants] are deprived of the advantages of fortune, the more they are entitled to the aid and favor of the magistrate, father of the country."[49]

Voicing an older, more traditional conception of honor, Feart, Duel's lawyer, argued that the honor of both the girl and her child was already irreparably damaged and that a marriage with a seducer would be even less honorable than a life of celibacy in the convent. In other words, completing the first phase of the dishonor was enough; it was the essence of the act, not its publicity, that mattered. He argued: "The sacred bonds of marriage can repair a mistake, but they should not crown a crime. . . ." A woman's honor cannot be restored by marrying her seducer/lover: "such an alliance would be a new opprobrium for demoiselle Duel. . . ." The marriage would be a sacrilege and "this profanity can only attract, for the guilty ones, the terrible vengeance of the God it outrages."[50] God, unlike the public, could not be fooled by a hastily concluded marriage. For Feart, the duties of the citizen were secondary to the respect due God's sacraments. In another place, he upholds other traditional values, including the ultimate nature of paternal authority: "One will call sir Duel's case the case of every father, of morality, of virtue, of religion, even more than his own case; every voice unites to demand that demoiselle Duel be returned to her father once and for all. . . ."[51] Paternal authority must be protected by the courts especially when it is unclear whether or not a daughter has consented to her own seduction. If she is innocent, then Henry should be condemned as a vile seducer; if complicitous, she is guilty of disobeying her father and must be punished.

Even corporally. The reference to Duel's suffering at the hands of her father may have been directed at the sentimental father-magistrate whose own paternity was evoked despite the degree to which he was above personal interest. Des Essarts recounted the violence to which Duel was subjected by her father; he was clearly an abusive father whose reckless rule needed to be checked by the legal system. No doubt this brutality made sensitive readers shudder, though certainly the court would have believed the abuse to be incidental to the issues at stake and neither Des Essarts nor Ader explicitly condemns the father's violence.

In fact, Feart argued that the bottom line was Henry's culpability, that even the issue of the girl's consent was irrelevant. He persisted, "rape by seduction should be punished still more severely [than that of violence] because it creates an accomplice out of an innocent victim."[52] Prosecuting a similar case, lawyer Castan de la Courtade explained that this is inevitably so: "It is only the first victory which costs a seducer: the will of his unfortunate victim will thereafter be his own: in such a way he subjugates her being, so that she can think only by his spirit, sense only by his heart, see only by his eyes. . . ."[53] In other words, a young woman in love was believed to be incapable of consent; once a "seducer" had inspired passion, she could no longer be held responsible for her behavior. The degree to which she was ignorant of the law went even further to prevent her accountability. Thus, young women were always already victims, deserving of pity, surely, but not of the public's scorn. Legal presumption of guilt should always rest with the man, argued another lawyer:

> Every time that it is a question of the seduction of a girl, one presumes that the man knows the laws because he violates them for his benefit; and one never presumes that the girl [knows them], because

> they are neglected for her fall; the one, audacious and free in his passion, conserves honor in the arms of pleasure; the other, in a passing delirium, finds an eternal shame. A man very studiously hides, from the eyes of a woman, these laws which would offend her modesty; and anyway a girl doesn't occupy herself with such grave subjects.[54]

The criminal retains his honor, while the victim is condemned to an eternal shame. Does this not render the concept "honor" meaningless? The girl who finds her honor lost, who is shamed in the eyes of the public, may, however, still retain her virtue—despite, in this case, voluntary sexual transgression. The lawyer invoking this premise to defend his client, a woman seduced and abandoned under a marriage promise, suggested that women's ignorance made them the easy prey of men. But would he have called for their education as a means of empowerment?

Probably not; rather, such arguments were used either to justify official involvement in relationships between men and women, or to strengthen paternal authority. This is why the court punished Duel's daughter by mandating her incarceration in a convent. Having in mind his daughter's best interest, a father would be the best qualified to determine his daughter's fate:

> This minor cannot dispose of herself. She doesn't have at all, in the eyes of the law, the degree of will necessary for consenting alone. It is necessary that her parents' view concurs with her own. Hence, since one can receive her only from them, taking her, without their first having given her, is to ravish her from them; it is stealing from them the dearest portion of their property; and in this sense it is a public crime.[55]

A young woman incapable of consent is not only dependent on her parents' will, but also is her parents' property to be disposed of as they see fit. Moreover, the seduction of a young woman is not only a crime against her parents' property, but a public crime, manifesting that the public is yet another party to which one must be accountable, that it, independent of the private individuals involved, can be offended and can therefore demand retribution. This is why Des Essarts and others questioned the hegemony of public opinion in conferring honor or shame: its verdicts were not always just, as case after case illustrates.

Defending the public as tribunal, Lawyer Fournel argued a case in 1787, which originated in circumstances similar to those between Duel and Henry, but in which the parents were eventually moved to grant their consent to the marriage between their daughter and her seducer/lover. However, Fournel insisted: "The rape having been denounced, the public minister cannot close his eyes to this outrage. The parents' desistance has the effect of reconciling their personal injury, but not the injury done to public order by a violation of one of the first duties of society. The parents' consent to the marriage of their daughter to the rapist is of no consideration, because this late consideration is obviously the result of necessity, and girls should not be obtained by force."[56] Here it is the indulgent parent, rather than the tyrannical one, who acts out of self-interest. Thus, regardless of their stance, parents' reactions to the transgressive behavior of their children must be scrutinized by magistrates uncompromised by self-interest. Once publicized, a violation of mores required a public settlement; this is why individuals and families attempted to conceal the sexual misconduct of their members. Yet concealment was the antithesis of virtue. Ultimately, women would have to be free from the weight of public scorn, rooted in tradition and group identity, to achieve modern identities in which their possession of virtue entitled them to autonomous action.

In the three cases considered in this chapter, abusive men find their power ambiguously checked by the decisions of the courts as lawyers called for the mitigation of male tyranny. Competing definitions of honor reveal the degree to which they were gender and class specific, and that Des Essarts consistently favored litigants who could claim to have less selfish and more natural interests. Advocating democratic notions of honor, Des Essarts and Barère challenged aristocratic hegemony in the Noailles' case, suggesting even that the letter of the law may be subverted if its implementation goes against the interests of society, in this case defined as the legitimation of a "marriage" that would resurrect the reputation of the virtuous bourgeoise Catherine Noailles. De Rois senior was both aristocrat and father; hence challenges to his authority have both anti-paternalism and antiaristocratism as subtexts, and hostility towards him had as much to do with his social class as his social role. The Martin case, on the other hand, featured a libertine aristocrat whose fatherhood is merely a footnote in this tale, interesting only to the extent that he rejected a social role which proved that his own behavior could merit dishonor unless concealed from the public. Martin's own all-but-absent (step)father played little part in this drama, his absence being a necessary plot device, yet his matrimonial strategy for his daughter implied complicity in her seduction. Conversely, in the Duel case, anti-paternalism can be separated from anti-aristocratism, in which a petite bourgeois father's traditional notions of honor were based on patriarchy, and not specifically rank. Duel's sacrifice of his daughter and grandson to a life of shame rested upon arguments that daughters are their fathers' property and that marriage after seduction cannot appease an outraged public. Yet, the sentimentalized representations of natural unions based on mutual attraction, found in two of these cases and echoing Rousseau and other Enlightenment writings on marriage, as well as fictionalized romances, eventually inform the language of legislation enabling divorce, ending arranged marriages, and destigmatizing illegitimacy. This explication of three *causes célèbres* then reveals the tenets of a defense strategy which defended the rights of wronged women and called for the diminution of forms of male power analogous to that held by the traditionally privileged, including the king.

Noailles and Martin affirmed their capacity for reason, autonomous action, and moral judgment. Noailles and Duel willfully engaged in illicit sexual behavior, defying patriarchy and then daring to defend themselves, offering, through their lawyers, a version of events which demonstrated their virtue, tormented by the corrupt self-interests of the men who would punish them. As women striving to achieve modern identities, each of the three women whose cases were featured in this chapter told her story and was vindicated by the representations of their stories which Des Essarts made public.

In the next chapter, fathers are largely absent and it is spousal relations which are politicized as women consistently win their suits for separation on the basis of their virtue. With paternal power itself no longer the specific target, and with courts largely agreeing with lawyers' positive representations of their female clients, it is possible to bring into sharper relief the possibilities of the liberatory moment represented by the *Causes célèbres.*

3

The Bonds of Matrimony: Separations

> Have we anything more precious than honor? It is still more so for those who have never lost it. How to require an honest spouse to continue intimate relations with a wretch whom laws have expelled from civil society and branded with ignominy? Is there a crueller and more miserable existence than this for a woman who has never neglected the duties of citizenship?[1]

In such a formulation, honor is linked to citizenship, and a virtuous woman is entitled to free herself from the source of her dishonor, namely her husband who happens in this case to be a galley slave because a convicted forger.

Marriage was the central act upon which the social contract was built, for it was within marriage that the future citizenry of the state was formed. Female sexual exclusivity was required in order to guarantee the legitimacy of that citizenry. Therefore, divorces were prohibited in France; annulments, in the case of non-consummation or impotence, were occasionally granted because propagation was impossible. Even convictions of serious offenses did not warrant divorce, and would be contested if presented as grounds for separation in and of themselves, as in the case alluded to above, a detailed explication of which will follow.[2] In general, however, separations were granted with increasing frequency throughout the eighteenth century. Des Essarts for one lamented the number of separations "which have multiplied to an incredible point"; in fact, in his collection, no single issue involving women was brought before the courts more frequently.[3] Speaking out against self-interest, he accounted for the increase in separations this way: "In happy centuries, when morals were still pure, one rarely saw divorces. Interest was not the principal agent behind the actions of men: it did not preside over marriages: it did not unite, with deadly and indissoluble ties, two incompatible souls."[4] This of course echoes the condemnations of paternal and aristocratic interestedness in the previous chapter. Based on his study of separations, Lottin also notes "a significant emergence of the problems of material interests which appear as one of the chief factors and catalysts for the breakup of couples."[5]

Separations were also scorned because, by failing to redress the origins of the problem, they provided no real solution. This is the principal reason they were under attack in the Old Regime and why they would be replaced by divorce during the Revolution. Des Essarts goes on: "Because of this difference [from the Romans] it follows that the form of divorce adopted by us entails a sort of contradiction, by separating in fact that which remains, however, really united and inseparable, and that it is only a violent remedy, introduced out of necessity, and out of the natural obligation to choose between the lesser of evils."[6] Because they continued to be legally married, neither spouse was free to make an appropriate use of his/her sexuality. And living separately could lead spouses into adultery. Thus, separations, which were often intended to restore one of the spouse's honor (usually the wife's), led to further dishonor, starting of course with the loss of honor that resulted from coming public with the private circumstances of a bad marriage. However, with a criminal for a husband, hiding dishonor from the public gaze was already impossible.

Typically in the *Causes célèbres*, separations were granted to women who were described as victims of their fathers' greed and/or their husbands' cruelty. Des Essarts likened the woman married off by her father to a man she does not love to a slave sold to the highest bidder: ". . . . reasons of convenience are the only ones [fathers] consult: he matches the fortunes and not the hearts of those to be chained to each other; . . . . I don't doubt it would outrage those fathers to be compared to unnatural men of commerce who, in more barbarous countries than ours, traffic in the blood and liberty of men." The cases in the previous chapter demonstrate the degree to which fathers sacrificed their children to their selfish interests. Des Essarts then goes on: "And is it not also another tyrant who, under the respectable title of husband, seizes his young victim, and chains her pitilessly in irons still more terrible because they are sacred, and because no hope of liberty either softens or consoles this species of servitude?"[7] Thus women were victimized twice: by the self-interested father whose marriage plans for his "chattel" took no account of her wishes, and by the husband who benefits from a servitude from which there was no escape.

Yet there were those who saw the "bonds of matrimony" as beneficial to women because they enchained men and women equally. Lawyers Martineau and Target considered the benefits and drawbacks of divorce in one famous case involving their Jewish clients, Piexotto and Acosta, respectively. Much like Des Essarts above, Martineau insisted that divorces achieved the benefits that justified the tolerance of so-called separations which were too weak to actually remedy the ills they purported to. He even cited Moses who tolerated divorce as a necessary evil: "He preferred repudiation to the secret murder of wives."[8] He then explained that Jews "regard celibacy as an outrage to the Creator, and a violation of the sacred laws of nature."[9] It is an illuminating coincidence that the legalization of divorce should follow one year after the Revolutionary Assembly granted Jews the privileges of citizenship in September 1791, and one year before the penalization of celibacy.

Target countered, interestingly enough, not with a defense of male privilege. Instead, he claimed that divorce was the worse of two evils, for it enabled a cruel man to victimize his wife even more: "Arbitrary, capricious, unjust, inspired by inconstancy and by licentious passions, this divorce is a weapon, which, when placed in the hand of the strongest, is destined only to strike the weakest; innocence unable to defend itself, virtue which is unable to sustain blows. . . . Of two beings created for a mutual happiness, one has all the privileges, the other is deprived of every right."[10] In this formulation, a woman does not merely possess virtue, but she is virtue itself; defenseless and innocent, virtue itself will be destroyed by a cruel tormentor, unless the law, and the father-magistrates who are its mouthpiece, offers protection. Lawyers agreed about male capriciousness and female vulnerability, but disagreed about the best means to protect virtue. For Target, giving men access to divorce would be just one more weapon in their arsenal. He speculated that a man who was merely bored with his wife, especially when she became elderly, would neglect his obligations to her and abandon her just when she needed him most. This male penchant for inconstancy was the main reason that other lawyers also supported the principle of indissolubility as a potent form of social control. The rhetorical question was thus posed: "is not the indissolubility of marriage a necessary check on us, a useful counterweight which balances and fixes the national fickleness?"[11]

As in the previous chapter, when women's ignorance of the law was seen to compound their vulnerability, no call for educating them was issued. Similar limits to the improvement of women's position can be seen in the debate on divorce. As Jeffrey Merrick puts it, lawyers "willingly credited women of the propertied and educated classes with moral sensitivity, rather than bestial appetites, but also deprived them of moral autonomy. . . . They defended the reputations of their clients, unjustly accused of misbehavior, without formulating a vindication of the rights of women as such."[12] While no collective vindication was advanced, lawyers did articulate an agenda, one woman at a time, which challenged the traditional justifications of male power on the basis of natural law and citizenship. Their narrative strategies contributed to a discourse which would enable the articulation of such a vindication within a decade. Vindicating one woman at a time, each of the following cases illustrates the degree to which a "certain emancipation of women" was achieved in the late eighteenth century.

In 1761, Marie-Thérèse de L., daughter of a public prosecutor in the royal court at Sables-d'Olonne, married J. L. Biaille de L., son of a chief clerk of court overseeing royal accounts in Nantes. Marie was richer than J. L., already the holder of a considerable amount of property, but her parents forced the marriage, lured by the title J. L. would inherit from his father. Here too it is an interested father, Marie's, who is the first guilty party. Thus Marie is already depicted as one of those young victims, not unlike the slave, whose fate is determined by a man's selfish interest.

Within 3 years, J. L. was condemned to the galleys in perpetuity for having "forged bills of sale for his profit, and of having bribed and intimidated witnesses." While he was awaiting sentencing in Paris, Marie voluntarily moved to the Sainte-Aure convent and then on to a boardinghouse. In the words of her lawyer:

> Such a lot of misfortunes for Dame de L.! She realized that, in spite of her own innocence, the shame with which her husband was about

> to be covered reflected back on to her, and that if this news became known in the Saint-Aure convent, she would be chased out in ignominy. To avoid this humiliation, she left and withdrew to a women's boardinghouse, taking the precaution of introducing herself by her family name.[13]

Her husband's crime entailed her loss of honor, a loss of honor which would be transferred to the people and institutions surrounding her. This suggests that honor, unlike virtue, was not inherent in the individual, but was the culmination of the public's recognition of one's virtue. So, she dropped her married name, thereby protecting her husband's honor as well, and took up lodging at another boardinghouse while attempting to solicit the help of influential people on his behalf; this in spite of the verbal abuse he heaped upon her every time she visited him in prison. She finally succeeded in obtaining for him a "liberté de préau," during which time he convinced her that he was innocent. Yet he also, during this time, beat her. Now pregnant and desperate, she finally filed for a separation on January 11, 1769.

On March 3, his punishment was mitigated to five years in the galleys and branding in public. After the branding, he was sent to Brest where he lived with a chambermaid who, he told everyone, was his wife. Marie used this newest outrage, "this scandalous and public abandonment of his legal spouse, this culmination of defamation and scorn" as further grounds for separation. It was this that finally moved the court to grant her request on June 8, 1774.

As Merrick pointed out above, "women of the propertied and educated classes" were esteemed by the courts to possess a "moral sensitivity." This justified their preferential treatment vis-à-vis women of the people who were regularly described as immune to blows, shrewish, and prone to violence themselves. Marie's lawyer asked: "How can a woman who possesses education and morals be returned to the arms of a galley slave?"[14] This is the same lawyer who described her in this chapter's opening passage "as an honest spouse who never neglected the duties of citizenship."

J. L.'s lawyer viewed the situation differently. Like Target's, his opposition to a woman's bid for independence was not expressed as a defense of patriarchy, but rather was based on the argument from male inconstancy. If men bring dishonor upon themselves, if they incur the scorn of public opinion, their wives must tolerate it and be consoled by the knowledge of their own virtue.[15] Even more, male disorders should not be rewarded in the form of liberating men from marriage, for their liberty would not only ruin their family's reputation for honor, it would render them dangerous even to society, if, as libertines, they seduced and abandoned multiple women. Women are obligated not only to tolerate their husbands' bad conduct, but also, as moral exemplars, to correct them: "It is because a man has weaknesses that it is important to give him a family obligated to tolerate [his weaknesses] out of duty. . . . This man has his resources in the household; he needs to be a husband and father. That isn't all: he even finds in these titles of father and husband powerful reasons to improve himself." In other words a dutiful wife will tolerate his disorders and will inspire him by her own good behavior to return to virtue. Because the man alone is not only interested but impassioned, "he finds in family relations that which establishes the union of external concerns and personal interest, which makes him regulate or vanquish his preferences. . . . It is above all because he has passions and depraved penchants that it is not good for a man to be alone."[16] The union of the external and the personal would be the basis for an enlightened self-interest; only the family man could vanquish his self-interest. And only the virtuous woman, more immune to passion, could curtail his selfishness.

Marie's lawyer did not accept that a wife could necessarily correct her husband. Implying women's weakness and inferiority, he suggested it might be the opposite: his bad example would corrupt her. This is an ironic twist in a defense which rested on her virtue, but he argued from general principle. "Should the law not fear that a wife who lives with the guilty one in a union will abandon finally the principles of honor and probity, vanquished, moreover, by the ascendancy of a vicious and dishonored husband?"[17] Des Essarts cited one such case to prove that "vice is contagious," especially among the poor and uneducated. The wife in question was very impressionable evidently, and Des Essarts insisted that from a virtuous husband she could have learned virtue. Instead she was her husband's accomplice in theft. When she inadvertently confessed to having stolen a sheep with him, the two were arrested. He murdered her in their cell in Beauvais in September, 1779. The moral of the story?

> Nature and laws give him such an irresistible ascendancy over the weak being that he has chosen for his companion that it is very difficult for a woman not to follow the example of the one who is supposed to regulate her conduct. A woman who has received a virtuous education, and who has principles, can retain the horror for crime that nature has inspired in her and can resist the dangerous example of her husband; but in the lower classes of society for whom existence is dependent on arduous and crude work, it is quite rare that a guilty husband does not succeed at familiarizing his wife with crime.[18]

Note here too that education makes all the difference—it distinguishes the virtuous woman from her counterpart in the lowest classes. The virtuous woman possesses a degree of autonomy essential to the establishment of modern identity. Should the poor woman, like her virtuous and educated counterpart, gain independence from her husband? No poor woman brought suit in the cases featured in the Des Essarts' collection, and as we shall see below, the modern individualism to which women were called in the late eighteenth century was class-specific. Perhaps this is why there were far more separations demanded by and granted to women of the bourgeoisie, and why there were more separations in the late eighteenth century than ever before, amounting to a "certain emancipation of women" in Lottin's phrasing. Apparently, even a nasty glance could so outrage such a delicate and sensitive woman that she would demand a separation from a man for whom she could no longer feel anything but loathing:

> well-born women, raised gently with tenderness, in the lap of comfort. . . . become delicate and sensitive. For such women nothing is without insult; a gesture, a look can be outrages. Often a single word indelibly imprints itself in her mind; it is less the words than the intention which offends her. From this can be engendered deep resentments and irreconcilable hatreds which make cohabitation odious and render a legal separation necessary.

For this lawyer, uncomfortable cohabitation was sufficient grounds for separation. Never mind adultery, brutality, or criminality. However, this sensitivity is not to be found in all women; it results from good upbringing and a virtuous nature. "Those born in baseness develop morals and a lifestyle in accordance with their low status. Accustomed from birth to crude language and the most distasteful behavior, blows from a brutal husband leave no trace of resentment in the wife's heart, and the most profound calm always succeeds these temporary storms."[19]

Class bias is one of the reasons that no sustained demand for women's rights was voiced by lawyers arguing *causes célèbres*. They advocated for their individual clients, who, in separation suits, were invariably bourgeois. At the same time, they participated in a discourse that placed education over rank and virtue over honor, a discourse which would have radical implications in the next decades. Moreover, while poor women were not featured in separation suits, they too, if in possession of a transparent virtue, could win favorable hearings in the cases that brought them before the courts, such as inheritance or legitimacy disputes (as was the case with Emerie whose plight opened this book), or accusations of infanticide or other violent crimes (as is the case in the following chapters).

Marie eventually won her suit. Her lawyer convinced the courts that she was too virtuous to be the wife of a philandering galley slave. In the next case, male brutality is even more pronounced and here, too, a wife is eventually liberated from her oppressor—in part because of her virtuous education.

Dame D.'s father was a cavalry captain, a self-made man, whose origins were "vulgar." Yet at the time of her marriage in 1785, her father was rich enough to provide her with a sizeable dowry, 15,000 livres. Protective of his money and his daughter, her father insured that "separation of property" was written into the marriage contract.

This was a source of outrage to the new husband, who had concealed his "depraved heart" with "seductive language" and an "advantageous exterior." In debt, and with a taste for luxury, he married her primarily for her money. Creditors, including a prostitute, were always after him. To repay his "whore," he stole from his new wife the medallion he had given her with his portrait, which his "whore" then sported around the Palais Royal. Des Essarts observed that this was such horror for a young wife, but that "other anguishes awaited her."[20] When his wife made "some observations in a modest and sweet tone" about his disorderly finances, he was unmoved by her "touching prayers and virtuous tears." Instead he menaced her and threatened to throw her out the window. Apparently, the beatings were regular, even when she was pregnant. He claimed that he beat her to be rid of her, and that he feared she would try to poison him.

Though she nearly died in childbirth, the child made her forget everything she had suffered, and she "burned with the desire to deposit her child in its father's arms." She hoped the child would soften him, but all he wanted from her was money. The abuses continued, and when the maid intervened, she too was beaten. Dame D. pitied him, knowing that his creditors would arrest him if she stopped protecting him and filed for separation. So she redoubled her efforts to win his love and took the child to him, herself sick and burning up with fever. Des Essarts interjected: "Ah! Doubtless, doubtless, this husband, until now insensitive, will be vanquished by the sublime and touching heroism of his virtuous companion."[21] But instead he rejected them both, in spite of the fact that she, in a supplicant posture worthy of Sophie, prostrated herself, weeping, and clutched his knees. Her virtue thus resided in her degree of self-sacrifice, her utter lack of self-interest. To please him, she finally put her child out to a wet nurse. Then he finally returned home, but one night shortly thereafter he literally threw her out of bed, saying he wanted it all to himself; their maid again intervened to her own peril when he went for his sword. He fired her immediately. Then he raped their new maid, after quelling her resistance by a thrashing with fireplace tongs.

The plight of these domestic servants merited no commentary on the part of Des Essarts or her lawyer, Chantereyne. The abuse they suffered is recounted only to vilify D. and to fill the catalogue of horrors Dame D. had to endure. Other instances of rape are described in the next chapter, but when the victims are poor, urban women, there is little commentary on the violence itself, suggesting that the class bias which insisted that poor wives were impervious to blows extended to the poor rape victim, a kind of disposable woman whose susceptibility to abuse was attributed to the vulgarity of the "people."

After mentioning the rape, the narrative resumes. In January 1786 he had to take refuge in the Temple, fleeing his creditors. Twice she obtained temporary reprieves of six months each for him, and finally got her father to obtain a suitable post for him, his interventions suggesting that he was a loving and compassionate father, unlike those in chapter one. To no avail; he continued his debauchery and reckless spending. One evening, while dining with her sister, mother, and grandmother, he demanded the keys to her desk. When she refused, he poured a bottle of ink over her head. He stopped due to her grandmother's intervention and took his violence out on the maid instead. He then attempted to isolate her from her family by proclaiming from a balcony at the Palais Royal where she was promenading with her mother that he would beat her mother if he saw them together again. And he lived up to his word by chasing after them with a log—they barely escaped. She confronted him one last time in the Palais Royal courtyard where he was flirting with his "whore." He would have choked her to death had passersby not intervened. Then she fled to her last refuge—a convent. His next strategy to terrorize her was to prevent her from seeing the child, but by March 17, 1787, when she finally brought her plight to the attention of the authorities, she was permitted to keep the child with her and he was barred from seeing her.

Finally, outraged by the number of women he brought home, and by his accusations that she was an adulteress, she brought her case before the magistrates in Paris while under her father's protection. Lawyer Chantereyne eloquently pleaded her case, but the court of Châtelet decided in her favor by default; her husband failed to file a countersuit and the separation was finally granted on January 8, 1788.

Even though his client's father was a mere cavalry captain, Chantereyne argued that Dame D. was too wellborn and bred to tolerate her husband's maltreatment: she was, after all, not a woman of the people: "these [mental] abuses are felt much more keenly by a wellborn woman, than are acts of violence by a woman of the people. These principles are so familiar to you, sirs, that it is not necessary to develop them."[22] This explains in part why there was no editorializing around the violence inflicted upon the maids. But it also illustrates that it was the character defamation, and not the violence, which more often moved judges to grant women's demands.

Ranking above the people entitled one to preferential legal treatment. Clearly, the law's application depended upon the litigants' class background, yet "class" often implied level of education. For example, one lawyer defeated a woman's request for separation not only because she was from the artisan class, but more because she and her husband lacked education:

> Among the people . . . a husband can express his anger in a most brutal way, but as long as this doesn't happen often, if his wife's life is not in danger, then Justice will always turn a deaf ear to her complaints. The law regards these domestic squabbles as passing storms which can always be attributed to the husband's lack of education as much as to his cruelty.[23]

Male brutality was believed to be a result of poor education—here defined as upbringing as well as intellectual training—just as female sensitivity to it was a product of a good education. What would be called inappropriate for the classes above the people was deemed normal behavior when litigants from the people brought their cases before the law. But note that the brutality inflicted upon Dame D. was not that of an ignorant brute. Presumably, her husband was from the same social class as she. Did education really reduce violence against women?

Though Chantereyne listed the husband's physical brutality as one of the justifications for separation, he did not attack the husband for this. Rather, he insisted:

> Of all the justifications for separation [added M. Chantereyne] the most valid is, without a doubt, the stain delivered by the husband to his wife's honor. Honor, a woman's sole possession, should be protected by her husband [guardian of her virtue]: it is he who should defend it. If fidelity is a woman's first responsibility, one cannot accuse her of having violated it without delivering a mortal blow to her honor. It is character assassination. . . .[24]

Blows to the body eventually disappear, but blows leveled against a woman's honor were mortal; any man might, in a moment of rage, physically brutalize his wife, but only a man with an "evil character" could attack her honor.[25] While her virtue may be intact (because she is not guilty of what she is accused), her reputation, her honor, is ruined. He accused her of adultery, of inappropriate sexual behavior, and in this he revealed not only his failure to protect her reputation, but also his disregard for public opinion. In so doing, he abused his authority to the point where he destroyed its basis: he could no longer call himself her husband.

A woman whose honor has been destroyed by her husband not only can, but must, file for a separation. If she does not express sufficient outrage at this attack, then the public will scorn her. One lawyer put it this way:

> But pity the woman who can witness without horror the theft of her honor, this repository so precious to her sex; if, insensitive to outrages, she is lax enough to concur with the view held by the one who defames her and covers her with shame, she is a vile creature who merits only scorn: trash of her sex she crawls ignominiously in shame and dishonor.[26]

Similarly, a husband's adultery should not be tolerated if its publicity threatened a wife's honor. Tolerance of public scandal convinced the public that she herself was not motivated to protect her own reputation for honor, that being her first duty as a citizen rated even higher than her duties to her husband. On the other hand, tolerance of private disorder, even adultery, is a "secret bitterness" she must endure. Chantereyne continued: "when the husband's infidelity, accompanied by scandal, announces, on his part, a disregard for his duties and all discretion; when it becomes a source of shame, mortifications, and outrages for the wife, one cannot require her to remain in such an insupportable situation."[27]

In other words, male adultery was not as acceptable as the leniency of the law suggests. "It was not the husband's adultery per se that was the offense, but the form of it that directly offended the wife's honor and sensitivity," observed Roderick Phillips in his comprehensive study on the history of divorce.[28] As was the case in many *causes célèbres,* the emphasis is on appearance and the maintenance of a sound reputation for honor by fooling the public. In both cases considered so far, the accusation was false; yet each woman was "dishonored." Once again, then, honor is revealed to be tentative, and unlike virtue, not intrinsic within the person but rather dependant upon reputation, which could be contrived. Affronts to a wife's reputation—which resulted from the publicity of the adultery, or even from a false accusation—provided the most irrefutable grounds for separation. Lawyer Godard put it simply in a similar case also featured in 1788: "One has thought with reason that if a woman, defamed by a stranger, has the right to prosecute it in criminal court, it is necessary that she at least have the feeble resource against her husband of demanding a separation when it is from him that the offense came."[29] Yet he knew that women had much to lose by coming public with their "troubles": "This wife has done, then, that which every honest and virtuous woman should do; she has recognized that a demand for separation is a real scandal; she did not want to set a precedent without a pressing necessity; she waited as long as she could until she was finally determined to tell the tribunals and the public of her troubles. . . ."[30]

In the case of defamation, a husband had already publicized his wife's alleged disorders; to clear her name she, too, would have to engage the public. A husband's adultery unaccompanied by scandal was permissible, or could be rectified privately, for as a rule, "the prosecution of the crime of adultery has the objective of watching over the interior of families, and not of avenging public order."[31] Thus once the public had been engaged, as was the case in the seductions prosecuted in the last chapter, a public settlement was required: these always favored the woman.

The circumstances and strategies in the two prior cases bear a resemblance to each other that borders on the cliché. Indeed, nearly every suit for separation of the more than three dozen featured in the *Causes célèbres* is a variation on the theme of female virtue tormented by male profligacy. Even when involving litigants as diverse as the Jewish and English couples briefly described earlier, cases revolved around stock characters in a predictable narrative. What these cases provided, however, was an opportunity for readers to consider the diverse customs of nondominant cultures as a mirror upon which to reflect those of the French. They also illustrate the degree to which Des Essarts posited a universal standard for gendered honor and virtue.

While lawyers on both sides of the Atlantic pleaded sympathetically and successfully for their virtuous and abused clients, more problematic female behavior yielded more ambiguous results. In the next very complex case, we see the plight of an aristocrat whose publicity of her illicit affair motivates a self-styled representative of the tribunal of public opinion to prosecute her. In this *causes célèbre* we return again to the most oft-cited reason for marriage breakdown, alliances based on the selfish interests of the parents. This case also, finally, addresses issues of paternity and maternity, heretofore omitted from considerations of marriage termination, a strange omission given the obsession with legitimacy which underpins marriage regulations to begin with. But then Marie and Dame D. were virtuous and even their libelous husbands did not deny paternity. With Alliot, it is a different story.

In 1752 in Lunéville, Monsieur Alliot, general commissioner and member of the King's council to King Stanislaus of Poland, arranged for his daughter Marie-Louise, aged twenty-three, to marry the son of de Pont, "conseiller" for the sovereign court of Nancy. Both children resisted the idea with all their might; the young man fled and the young woman attempted to kill herself. Both sets of parents responded with threats of disinheritance and other, more brutal, forms of punishment. The young woman even begged to be sent to a convent. To his daughter, Alliot proclaimed: "No, miss, you will not go to a convent; you would be too happy there. I will keep you at home: you will lack everything here. You will be the most miserable creature, and your room will serve as your prison until you obey me."[32] With such language, Alliot has distinguished himself as the most absolutist and tyrannical of fathers—not unlike Catherine Noailles' father-in-law. His regulation of her conduct, his imposition of his will on her sexuality, fits the stereotype of the self-interested aristocrat.

Finally the marriage was celebrated, but the bride alleged that she refused to allow it to be consummated; after a brief period of cohabitation with de Pont in Nancy, she ran away to a convent which refused to admit her without the consent of either her husband or parents. At this point her more indulgent mother convinced her cruel father to recognize his error and take her back. After this reconciliation between parents and daughter, eight years passed with no contact between the estranged spouses.

On January 3, 1760, the young de Pont filed for an annulment at the officiality of Toul. No motives were cited for this action. In the meantime, demoiselle Alliot had become the lover of the Chevalier de Beauvau. Their liaison resulted in the birth of a child, a boy (Basil Amable, one of the few children in the *Causes célèbres* referred to by name), whom Beauvau wanted to legally acknowledge as his own. To facilitate this, demoiselle Alliot filed a separate demand for annulment six weeks later, after having given birth on January 11 in Paris. Their son was baptized as the natural son of herself, demoiselle Alliot, and the Chevalier de Beauvau. Beauvau signed a promise to marry her once the annulment was granted which would thereby make their son legitimate.

Here the plot thickens. There were unidentified interested parties who did not want this baby to become the legitimate son of Beauvau. The text never is clear about who these people were. Perhaps there was a rival heir to either Beauvau's or de Pont's fortune. Whoever they may have been, Des Essarts described their method: "They searched among the people for some intelligent and audacious soul who would sell his talents to the passions of someone else."[33] Larrauld was such a man. Described merely as a "bourgeois de Paris," he was the spokesperson for a group of six others who believed themselves to be "charitable and wise reformers of public order." With the entrance into this case of Larrauld—this man of the bourgeoisie, this defender of "public order"—the sexual behavior of the aristocracy is checked by a reformer who insisted that he alone was free from the taint of self-interestedness.

With the aid of their lawyer, Le Gouvé, Larrauld and his coterie intended to prove that the boy was either the legitimate son of de Pont and his legal wife, or an adulterine bastard. Demoiselle Alliot hired Loyseau as her defense attorney. A legal battle ensued which revolved around the law's definition of legitimacy.

In France, both law and religion required that consummation occur for a marriage to exist; this is why "marriages" in which one party was impotent were annulled. To force a fertile spouse to live with an impotent partner would be, in effect, to waste his/her potential for being useful to the state. In cases of alleged impotence, courts required proof before they would annul the marriage. Such "proof" could only be obtained by medically examining the accused. Yet, these examinations were offensive to morals. One lawyer decried the "discursive explosion" around intimate matters like impotence.

> Impotence is a matter that the impurity of the last centuries has made quite public, and which has brought into use remedies which are perhaps worse than the problem. They were assuredly unknown in the first centuries, where such things were treated with more innocence and good faith. . . . The ordinances of our kings have never touched on such a dirty matter, to which one brought only tolerance and not authority.[34]

But times were changing and the medicalization and politicization of sexuality was already well underway by the time of the Alliot case to the degree that public citizens like Larrauld forced public discussion of private matters, and demanded that the regulation of sexuality be brought under the jurisdiction of the state.

In cases of impotence, proof could be obtained. But in Alliot's case, there could be no proof—only the testimonies of the bride and the groom. This is why Larrauld insisted that legal procedures be privileged over consummation in validating a marriage, because they were infallible and certain, whereas the sex act was surrounded by "a thousand clouds." As Le Gouvé put it:

> The conception of an infant is covered in darkness, a thousand clouds can obscure his origin; passions can bear their fatal influence there. It is necessary, in the midst of obscurities, to fix steadfast rules which, in maintaining the honor of marriages, and in presuming that there has been an absolute conformity to the purity of morals, guarantee at once the happiness of individuals and general tranquility.[35]

Formerly, archaic traditions, like the gathering of witnesses around the marriage bed and the required presentation of the blood-stained cloth the morning after, evolved to guarantee that consummation had in fact occurred. "Steadfast rules" did not necessarily mean laws. And while these usages were disappearing amongst the educated classes whose greater civility involved a greater degree of privacy, the people continued to have their own methods.

In Alliot's case, women undressed her and put her to bed on her wedding night, and then waited, listening, outside. It is reported in Des Essarts' account that when left alone, she screamed "the most piercing cries" and resisted physically, trying "to repulse the hands which stripped her."[36] After that she fainted, and the women heard nothing for one hour. Larrauld suggested that no one will ever know what happened during that hour, and therefore, only "steadfast rules" established in law are certain: the couple must be assumed to be legally and actually married. The boy born to Alliot, therefore, must belong to her husband or else be the fruit of adultery. "According to the law, more believable than them, he has no other father than M. de Pont," insisted Larrauld.[37] He then explained why the two would lie, why their account of their intimate lives should not be taken for truth: Alliot was the adulteress inflamed by a "criminal passion," and de Pont was a spineless cuckold, resigned to the fact that his wife did not want him, willing to sacrifice his son's legitimacy for her debauchery.

Larrauld, as a disinterested member of the public and as a Frenchman, believed that he must intervene on the child's behalf: "France, the asylum and country of this child, should give him all that it can. It is in France that his baptismal act has been falsified. It is France which must rectify the altered truth."[38] He privileged not just the general good over personal interest, but explicitly pointed to a national interest that must transcend all others. He argued that the fact of the child's birth proved that the marriage had been consummated, and he reminded the court that, "as judge, it must doubt; and in doubt the physical presumption must carry weight."[39]

Le Gouvé attempted to move the judges by raising their suspicions about Alliot's honor. It was she who was depicted as worse than self-interested; indeed, she was a slave to her passions and was willingly ruining herself, her husband, and especially her son. The adulteress who reveals her crime to the public makes a mockery out of her husband, and casts doubt upon the legitimacy of her offspring, making her an "unnatural mother"; still worse—she disrupts society itself: "Of all the ills which plague the order and harmony of society, the profligacy of women is surely the deadliest; such a woman disturbs every aspect of the state; her disorders lead to depopulation."[40] In a state increasingly worried about the size and quality of its population, these words carried weight.[41] The state could count Alliot's child the legitimate son of de Pont, and could thereby include him in the highest ranks of its population. Or it could believe the words of this adulteress and condemn the innocent to be an adulterine bastard:

> If a woman has been capable of violating her faith, let her mourn her infidelity in silence; let this remorse be her first chastisement: but let her not spread this punishment to her innocent son, in whom the wise policy of the law wants neither to perceive, nor presume, nor suspect the stain that the futile indiscretion of the mother can odiously reveal. Tranquility, the harmony of the entire society depends on the observation of these great maxims.[42]

Larrauld is asking Alliot to conceal her affair with Beauvau, even if it means granting legitimacy to an adulterine bastard—the maintenance of appearances being Alliot's chief obligation. Taken to its logical conclusion, this view has ironic consequences: the possibility for an adulterine bastard to even exist is precluded, if every child born to a married woman is by definition her husband's offspring.

Typically in adultery cases, it was the dishonored husband who demanded justice: "It is for the purpose of avenging the violated honor of the husband that these laws were armed with severity."[43] But in this case, the legal husband makes no claims to Alliot's fidelity; in fact he was the first to demand the annulment of their marriage on the grounds of nonconsummation. So clearly an individual's authority and privilege as a male is not at stake, an individual husband's honor has not been insulted. Larrauld was not interested in de Pont; he claimed he was only interested in the child: "This child is the child of the fatherland. His actual father then is the magistrate of the place where he was born, there is his protector."[44] The child belongs to the fatherland; biological fathers are eclipsed in importance, as the connection between the individual and the state becomes more direct. Between the citizen and the state there should exist no intermediary. All that matters is that the citizen is really a citizen. Therefore, says Larrauld, France owes the boy "all that it can give him." Representatives of France—magistrates who were father figures—are obliged to protect his legitimacy: "The most precious of all possessions is status, is legitimacy: status is, so to speak, a portion of ourselves. I am born under the law of marriage: thus I am born the son of my mother's husband. This is the title the laws give me. *Pater is est quem nuptiae demonstrant.* Whoever tries to steal this precious title is a ravisher; he is necessarily a criminal."[45]

Parents, because the secrets of the marriage bed belong only to them, do not create the child's legitimacy; the law does. By removing parents from this most important rite of passage—the entrance into civil society—the law can guarantee that it will have as many legitimate citizens as the state requires. The law's function is to dissipate the obscurity surrounding all acts which bear on a citizen's legitimacy; the adherence to "steadfast rules" makes the inappropriate behavior of the individuals in question increasingly irrelevant. The line between the citizen and the state is its most direct when only the law is the truth, and when the authority of intermediaries, even fathers, is eclipsed. Yet the consequences are inimical to virtue whose very transparency would make steadfast rules obsolete.

The parlement of Paris condemned Larrauld's actions and ordered him to pay the court costs on June 17, 1761. Alliot and de Pont were ordered to go before the judges of Toul, their "natural" judges, to pursue the annulment of their marriage. At Toul their request was denied, and the marriage was upheld as valid.

Though Larrauld's intervention in the case was declared invalid by the parlement of Paris, the ruling at Toul justified his position. The marriage between Alliot and de Pont was upheld as legally valid, in spite of the fact that both spouses swore, independently, that they had not consummated it. In this case, the observance of legal formalities, however, was all that was required to make a marriage, whereas in canon law consummation was the central factor legitimizing a union; in fact, in some cases, consummation without the necessary civil proceedings was enough to validate a union—this was Barère's claim in the Noailles' case. This privileging of the civil over the sacred, or even the natural over the civil, as in the Noailles' case, anticipates the redefinition of marriage as a legal contract that was advanced during the Revolution, and before, in the Toleration Edict of 1787 which recognized Protestant marriages as legitimate.

Yet the parlement of Paris did not accept Larrauld's argument and his claims were dismissed. But at Toul magistrates attested to the validity of the marriage. Did the latter judgment cancel out the former? Did the parlements have a slightly different agenda from the lower courts? Loyseau, Alliot's lawyer, dismissed Larrauld's claims as "dark absurdities," and asked what "secret enemies" were paying him. His rhetoric against Larrauld moved the courts to rule against this "agent."

Des Essarts also sided with Alliot, favoring transparent virtue over legality, calling her so-called marriage "a union formed by violence," referring to the young bride and groom as "victims" who were "sacrificed" to their parents' vile interests. He claimed that even the public condemned the two families, and thereby continued advocating increased independence for children from tyrannical fathers, especially in marriage choices.[46] Such independence would have prevented this whole sordid affair from happening in the first place. By portraying them as victims, Des Essarts wanted to help his readers understand why Alliot fell for Beauvau, the man who opened this poor woman's heart to love for the first time. In his rhetoric he is clearly participating in the cult of sensibility, pulling the heartstrings of readers who might otherwise be unsympathetic. He pressed her case even further and said she should not be punished for telling the truth, for wanting to secure her son's legitimacy by marrying his real father. He accepted that the law must have its unflinching precepts,

> But what! because the perspective of public order deems that the law take no account of the humiliating confession of the woman should this woman be found guilty for acquitting her conscience? That the magistrates, who see only general consequences, force a spouse to adopt the children of another is a misfortune that common cause demands; it makes a victim of public opinion who must obey the law. But is it for her who has betrayed marital faith to instigate this scandalous adoption? The law which doubts cannot presume misconduct; but the woman who knows the truth, is she punishable for not acting in accordance with the law?[47]

Law and public order act in concert here, one necessitating the other's existence. Though their joint mandates are meant to be inflexible, Des Essarts presumed that Alliot was telling the truth, and concluded that the law would be committing a graver error by suspecting the validity of her claim than by accepting it as true. Yes, "common cause" or public order mandated that all children born to Alliot would legally be de Pont's. But this creates a "scandalous adoption" that Alliot tried to prevent. She spoke the truth in spite of the shame it heaped upon her. The individual—even a woman—who knows the truth is obliged to stand against the law and public order so that real justice may be done by magistrates who normally see only general consequences, but in this case must respect her testimony. After all, the publicity of her illicit sexual activity with Beauvau was an act of self-sacrifice on behalf of her son whose legitimacy warranted her coming public. Such sacrifice was the essence of virtue.

Des Essarts would conclude, then, along with Alliot's lawyer Loyseau, along with the parlement of Paris, that Larrauld's attempt to attribute the child's paternity to de Pont was inappropriate. But the parlement's unwillingness to comment on the validity of the marriage adds just another ambiguous verdict to those considered so far. It did not want to admit Alliot's truth-telling as a basis for legislation. Empowering her to reveal the truth would come later—during the revolution—when illegitimacy was no longer upheld as a category for discrimination, and when virtuous transparency was upheld over honorable dissimulation.

The severance of ties between couples was increasingly common in the late eighteenth century precisely because courts were listening more favorably to complaints of abuse when they were made by virtuous women. Dame D. and Marie de L. possessed virtue and were thereby protected by father-magistrates when their own largely absent fathers were unable to do so. Lawyers persuasively argued that domestic despotism lacked legitimacy and that therefore, virtuous women were empowered to challenge it. Alliot, of questionable virtue, and an aristocrat, was more problematic. Though Des Essarts as narrator expresses sympathy for her position, he does not condemn the courts for their contradictory verdicts. Still, in all three cases, badly made marriages are condemned, and debates about the nature of marriage itself, stimulated in part by the prominence of "social contract" theory, underpin all of them and result in the ultimate de-sacramentalization of marriage. In all three, each woman is vindicated as an autonomous actor more capable of reason and moral judgment than the unreasonable, self-interested, and brutal men who tormented her virtue. But such a vindication could not be generalized to all women because of persistent prejudices based on status and especially level of education. This narrative of liberation was not undercut by a call for separate spheres as much as it was by class prejudice.

In the next chapter, shame before the tribunal of public opinion, resulting from the conception of an illegitimate child, causes the virtue of ordinary women to be suspected. Yet they too are represented as capable of autonomous action and moral judgment. However, in chapter four, aristocratic profligacy is not the cause of illegitimacy. Rather it is rape.

4
Atrocious Prejudices: Rapes

> How many examples prove with what obstinate pig-headedness the people have sometimes held atrocious prejudices against someone whom they formerly revered with such a servile and superstitious respect that they would never have interrogated that one's life nor suspected her virtue![1]

According to Des Essarts, the people were unable to recognize, let alone possess, virtue. Superstition, prejudice, servility, and pig-headed obstinacy meant that the people would readily turn against someone they had formerly idolized; they did not possess an objective gaze. In this instance, the Parisian crowd turned against an actress who was accused of poisoning her younger sister, Augustine, because of professional rivalry. Ever the conspicuous starlet, demoiselle Sophie Dufayel subjected herself to the panoptic lenses through which the public viewed her. "Women of the theater have the good fortune and the misfortune of always being under the eyes of the public; nothing is lost either for or against their reputations."[2] Ever the actress, it was only when real-life tragedy tore away her veil of appearances that the people thought they saw the real woman. The people now called for the execution of their former idol, "seeing" her for what she really was. This excitability and even bloodlust is what made the people suspect—their verdicts about others were as likely to be ignored as their complaints against each other. And yet, when the people constitute the public, their power to confer honor or shame motivates rich and poor to avoid their gaze through subterfuge, dissimulation, and a retreat from the street.

Arlette Farge has described a world—eighteenth-century Paris—in which privacy was virtually impossible: "One of the contexts of honor resides, in effect, in the constant contact between families and communities, in this indistinction between private and public life. It is this omnipresent gaze which procures knowledge about another and the right to talk about him."[3] This was at least as true, perhaps even more so, of eighteenth-century Languedoc. According to Nicole Castan: "Nothing, not even thefts or clandestine childbirths, can really remain hidden in these panoptic societies where anonymity scarcely exists."[4] In other words, *causes célèbres* among the people were almost always inescapable: the public was always already engaged.

Farge and Castan write principally about the "people," or, more specifically, the urban artisan class. But definitions of honor, and the strategies for constructing and maintaining reputations were different, however, for various social groupings, and depended greatly on their material circumstances. David Garrioch remarks that by the late-eighteenth century, the bourgeois lifestyle contributed to this differentiation: "His [the bourgeois'] form of prudery, like the woman's, required a home in which privacy was possible, and like hers involved a withdrawal from the life of the street."[5] Only in the private sphere could the "homo clausus" be effectively constructed.[6] But did the bourgeois women's retreat into the private sphere necessitate an irreversible retreat, thus exacerbating a double standard as the "public" was constructed to the exclusion of women?

The conflation of the terms "public" and "people" will be explored throughout this chapter. The "public," coming into being in the last decades of the Old Regime, was masculine-identified and bourgeois; it was made up of enlightened individuals; yet when those individuals disappeared into the masses, they could become a mob, not unlike the people. The people was feminine-identified and not bourgeois, by definition; it was made up of a faceless, nameless mob. Individual members of the public were transparent and discriminating while the people was reckless and anonymous. Mona Ozouf boldly states, "[T]he public is not the people, the latter being always inclined towards elusive and inflammable error."[7] The public was definitely not the "people," but as Keith Baker points out, the "public" remained ill-defined until the 1790s.[8] Like the virtuous women represented favorably in *causes célèbres* education was required for membership in the public. As Roger Chartier shows, the "public," as it emerged in "modern political culture" was made up, from its inception, of men who were "éclairés" and was "exclusive of all popular participation."[9] The "public" was conceived, therefore, as a society of "equals": a society of educated, liberal-minded *men* who were decidedly not the "prince" or his favorites.[10] Des Essarts maintained the distinction between the "public" and the "people," advocating the restriction of membership in the public to reasoning, enlightened individuals and excluding "the people who never reason" yet did not conclude therefore that public opinion was always correct either. Ultimately, only the lone individual, free from the scrutiny of either the public or the people, would be able to achieve modern identity.

Thus she who stands alone must possess a transparent virtue. In the case of Dufayel, Des Essarts knew that in spite of her now sullied reputation, or even her professional talent for artifice, she was good: "Gay, frivolous, and un-self-conscious, one knows after an hour of conversation with her that she absolutely lacks the passions and the character which lead to crime or which are linked to it." He cites her "naive and touching sensibility" and the charms of her youth (she was eighteen years old) and gender. She too exploits these charms in her own deposition: "In the midst of those follies which occupy a young actress, one does not acquire this vigor of resolve and this depth of character to even be able to imagine committing the crime of poisoning."[11] He published her memoir to vindicate her reputation, to restore honor to her name. It was her honor, not her virtue, which was blemished by the false accusation; her virtue, being innate, was inalterable. Because the theater can be a vehicle for the inculcation of virtue, actresses like Sophie were invaluable: "Unfortunately this profession which can inspire the lessons of virtue and respect for charity . . . is only too often the school of vice and seduction."[12]

The ability to discern the subtle distinction between honor and virtue, especially in actresses, was absent in the people. Still, Des Essarts recognized a kind of logic behind the verdicts and practices of the people. For example, he condemned the practice of charivari—the quintessence of popular ritual—as an "orgy of the people," but, "one will find some reason, well or ill founded, in custom. . . . The people set themselves up then as a public censor. . . . [But] the people use it, like it uses everything when it becomes a mob, without reservation and without distinction."[13]

This public censor could have positive implications; after all, the people punished those transgressions which offended the laws of nature (such as marriages between the very old and the very young)—even the people have standards for appropriate sexual behavior. Despite the people's occasional ability to act as a force for social control, for educated bourgeois like Des Essarts, the state was responsible for regulating transgressive behaviors; indeed, he praised it for eradicating charivari. Moreover, in contrast to the collective behavior of the people, the individual was admonished to practice the self-control of the "homo clausus." Privately and alone the "homo clausus" becomes civilized; only in him could virtue be effectively embodied. Yet the very privacy required for such civility allowed for dissimulation, the opposite of transparency.[14]

Because it acted spontaneously and collectively, by contrast, the people would never become civilized. Violence was just their way of life; it merited no attention when it occurred amidst the "people," as long as they victimized each other. "An ordinary row between common people followed by baton blows is a thing so frequent that one doesn't pay it the least attention; however, if the parties are of an honest and distinguished rank, one is shocked that education and sentiments have not preserved them from such a scandalous outburst."[15] Similar comments about the ability of education to inspire self-control and virtue informed the arguments of lawyers whose female clients sued for separation in the previous chapter, and won, because of their degree of civility.

Yet even such clearly virtuous women as Dames D. and L. were not immune to public scorn. Indeed, the precariousness of honor has been illustrated in every case considered thus far. Conferred from without, honor is a public acknowledgment of one's virtue. A woman seduced and abandoned, as was the case with Noailles and Martin, bears the shame of having yielded her virginity under a false promise. A woman in love with the wrong man, as was the case with Duel and Alliot, chooses her fate but is still vulnerable to the self-interested men who might shame her by publicizing her "fault." Even married women saw their honor compromised by the licentious and sometimes criminal behavior of their husbands. They alone bore the responsibility for restoring their honor by separating themselves from the source of their shame. Yet such a restoration was all but impossible since a *causes célèbre* entailed public scandal. Thus the people and the public, prone to error, could ignore virtue while being obsessed with honor, even in the case of violent rape where no questionable behavior on the part of the victim leaves her honor suspect.

"Rape is an attack against the modesty of a woman whose honor is ravished by violence or by artifice, such as drunkenness induced by a potion."[16] In this formulation, an act of violence robs a woman of her honor and the possibilities for restoring it are far more limited than for the other women we have studied. The loss of virginity is coterminous with a loss of honor, and without honor the opportunity for functioning as a citizen was foreclosed. Thus rape leads to the "civil death" of its victim. In Magdeleine Beaumont's case, rape, exacerbated by character defamation, leads to physical death as well.

Magdeleine Beaumont was the oldest of seven children. All of her life, she lived in a modest Parisian neighborhood next door to the Chevaliers, whose head-of-household was a petite bourgeois merchant, like her father. She was eighteen when Chevalier's son developed a passion for her. He assumed they would marry, given the similarity of their backgrounds, and their historical familiarity with each other. But Magdeleine's mother would not hear of it, desiring for her daughter a more prestigious match, and aware of Chevalier's "vicious inclinations."

In the panoptic society of an urban petite bourgeois neighborhood, Magdeleine was subjected to the young Chevalier's voyeuristic gaze. Angered by her rejection of him, he watched Beaumont's house closely early in 1779, and when Magdeleine was alone, he raped her during three hours of violence. In his narrative, Des Essarts consistently treats rape and dishonor as synonyms. Painting a chilling and tear-jerking picture of the rape, he reveals his sympathies:

> The cries of his victim were not heard; her tears, far from deterring her persecutor, only hastened the moment of her dishonor. Three hours passed in this combat. It was only after such a lengthy resistance, after having exhausted herself, after nearly tearing from its hinges the fatal door which opposed her flight, that, desperate, languishing, she succumbed and the cruel one enjoyed his victory."[17]

With such precise details like the "door nearly torn from its hinges," Des Essarts indulges his readers' voyeurism. Not only was Magdeleine subjected to Chevalier's gaze, she would eventually be seen by the public, the law, and masses of readers.

Des Essarts' inclusion of vivid details serves other purposes. This depiction of the brutality of Chevalier in this warlike "combat" casts Magdeleine as a worthy opponent as well as an innocent victim: it is impossible to allege her complicity. Thus from the start she is to be pitied. Her father found her, and in his rage, thought only of avenging his daughter, but knowing that prosecuting Chevalier through the courts would entail making public, and would thereby complete, Magdeleine's dishonor, he refrained from reporting the rape to the authorities. Not only would Magdeleine's honor be irretrievably lost should the episode become public, but, as another lawyer arguing a similar case pointed out:

> [A]ll the tribunal's power cannot restore the honor of a victim of seduction or brutality. Reduced to pass the rest of her days in celibacy, this status will be, for her, a perpetual reproach of her misery, and will remind her, every minute of her life, of the humiliation to which she has been condemned, which bars forever the hope of achieving the dignity of a wife.[18]

Because a woman's reputation was constructed by the public, law courts could do nothing to save a rape victim from the perpetual shame, loneliness, and fruitlessness of this fate. Keeping the affair private, then, became Beaumont's goal. He decided to accept the offer of Chevalier, "who, despite his crime, still retained some sentiment of honor" to marry her.[19] Chevalier, aware that rape was a capital crime, was willing to repair the damage by marrying her—obtaining through force what her mother had denied him. Magdeleine's reputation could be saved if a marriage could be hastily concluded, so her parents gave their consent.

Note that even the brutal rapist is moved to act out of a sense of honor, here too defined as appropriate sexual behavior. Would his reputation also be ruined by a *causes célèbre*? Nicole Castan offers an answer: "For men, sexual liberty is not unconditionally acceptable; on the contrary, a solid reputation in this sphere rather glorifies the young man. Humiliation comes, on the other hand, from a woman's rejection; it touches on the most sensitive honor of the man and often of his family."[20] Indeed Chevalier was acting out of a sense of honor; his rape of Magdeleine could be seen as an extreme demand for satisfaction after the insult of being spurned. The publicity of the rape, therefore, would disgrace him as well. A marriage would prevent the publicity of his rejection. But if fear of further dishonor was not enough to force him to save Magdeleine, "religion, the abuse he exercised towards this girl, and the lack of respect he has had for her oblige him in his soul and conscience to marry her. . . ."[21]

Now pregnant, Magdeleine even consented to the proposal, concerns about the legitimacy of her offspring overriding her own horror at the thought of sharing bed and table with Chevalier. She wanted to "assure the status of her children for whom, in spite of the outrage of which they were the fruit, she already felt the powerful emotions of nature."[22] She was willing to sacrifice herself in order to fulfil her duties as mother, thus revealing her lack of self-interest, the defining characteristic of virtue. Emphasizing the natural force of maternalism was one way lawyers moved the courts and Des Essarts moved his readers; the pitied innocent victim was also heroized. So: "She went to see the young man who had cruelly outraged her, it is true, but who had reduced her to the necessity of pardoning him; the dishonor with which she is covered in the eyes of the world force her to accept him as husband. . ."[23] Here dishonor is obviously something which is conferred by the public.

From the beginning, Chevalier's father refused to consent to the marriage, and threatened the young man if he did not retract his offer. The text is vague as to his reasons, but Isabelle Vissière in her brief commentary on this case suggests that Magdeleine might have been the fruit of an adulterous encounter between Chevalier's father and Magdeleine's mother, a marriage between the two children thereby being incestuous.[24] So strong was the father's opposition that he threatened his son into retracting his promise: "if his son wanted to preserve his good will, if the paternal home is dear to him. . . ."[25] The son agreed to retract, forcing Magdeleine to bring her story to the attention of the law. Obeying the 1556 edict that unmarried pregnant women go before the magistrates to make their "déclarations de grossesse," Magdeleine declared her pregnancy, naming Chevalier the father on October 1, 1779.[26] On the 15th he was arrested.

To exonerate his son, the elder Chevalier encouraged his son to deny his paternity, and allege that Magdeleine was a "vile prostitute." The woman must be scorned instead of pitied. Intimidated, the younger Chevalier asked a friend, Dupont, to testify that he, too, had

had sex with Beaumont, and that, therefore, no paternity could be proven. This public defamation would complete the act of dishonor which had begun with the rape. By insinuating that her honor was not intact before he raped her, Chevalier thereby negated the very existence of the rape, which was, by definition, a dishonoring of the victim. In other words, if a victim had no honor to be "ravished," then no rape could legally be said to have occurred.

In fact, legal discussions of whether or not a rape had occurred revolved around considerations of the victim's reputation for honor. Des Essarts said elsewhere: "But if the woman who complains was a prostitute, or even if she did not have an honest reputation, one cannot take her at either her words or her oath, regarding the violence of which she complains. . . ."[27] This resembles the reasoning used to grant virtuous women separations while "turning a deaf ear" to the complaints of women of the people. He then points out that the Romans did punish the rapists of *former* prostitutes, and of concubines who had lived with only one man. Rapes of prepubescent girls deserve the greatest punishment because their victims are "forever deprived of any hope of establishing themselves honestly and because these girls bring shame on their whole family even if [the violence they suffered] was not their fault."[28] Even though Chevalier's attempt at defamation failed (Dupont testified that Beaumont was virtuous and that Chevalier had bragged to him about the rape), her shame and its consequences would never be erased.

Magdeleine literally could not tolerate Chevalier's offense to her honor. With no hope of legitimacy for her offspring, she died fourteen days after giving birth to twin daughters on January 15, 1780. Chevalier continued to deny responsibility, and Magdeleine's father cared for the one infant that survived until the court appointed an adoptive father. On July 21, 1780, Chevalier was finally ordered to pay an annual pension for the child's rearing, and a sum (3,000 livres) in damages to the Beaumonts.

The law was not enough to save Magdeleine; according to Des Essarts it was public opinion that sealed her fate and sounded her death knell:

> She is innocent in her own eyes, and in those of her kin as well as in the eyes of the law, but is she in the eyes of the world? The more her virtue is pure, the more she fears the shadow of crime which has

> tainted her; the defamation to which she has been delivered removed her last hope, the sad consolation of being pitied. . . . She died on 15 January, 1780, after much suffering, surrounded by the tears of her devastated family, a victim of opinion and of someone else's crime.[29]

A woman's reputation was made or destroyed by public opinion, and upon this reputation rested her life. Despite her innocence and virtue, once her reputation was tarnished, once she was ravished of her honor, nothing could save her. Though Chevalier's charges of debauchery had been rejected by the courts, having raised the suspicion *publicly* was enough to ruin Magdeleine's reputation.

Significantly, the text does not indicate whether or not Chevalier was ruined by the crime that he perpetrated, and the sentence he received (to pay for his child's rearing and to compensate the Beaumonts financially) reveals that the court did not believe his actions warranted his expulsion from society, though a conviction of rape could lead to the death penalty.

The severity of the death penalty was intended to deter "libertines who take pleasure in rape." "The terrifying idea of the scaffold will calm [the would-be rapist's] senses and force him to respect morals." These remarks opened a case in which a six-and- a-half year old girl was raped by a day laborer. Aubert, who lived at Dunois at Châteaudun, was known as a "dangerous satyr." He raped Marie-Anne Pillaux; neighbors heard and had him arrested. His first judges condemned him to the galleys for life and 1000 livres in damages, but the public minister appealed to the parlement of Paris and secured a sentence of hanging on February 1, 1785. Des Essarts applauded the harsher sentence because only a "monster" would rape a child; such "monsters" could not be punished too severely and should above all be removed from society.[30]

As long as his victim was not prepubescent, however, after the deed was done, deterrence having failed, a rapist could avoid the death penalty by marrying his victim, creating an apparently legitimate family. But once Magdeleine was dead, there was no legitimate family left to constitute and invoking the death penalty made no sense. Besides, unlike Magdeleine, Chevalier, having behaved inappropriately in this sphere, had other roles to play which demanded honorable behavior. Perhaps he could make up for his crime.

In a similar case committed in the countryside, however, justice was meted out. "This crime is not common in the great cities where prostitution is regarded as a necessary evil, but in the heart of the countryside can still be found monsters who dare attack timid virtue." Thus again rape is defined as an attack on virtue itself, not just upon the individual victim. Jeanne Delaste possessed charms and a freshness that inspired passions. "Her fatal beauty would be an endless source of tears for her." She was a poor and virtuous shepherdess who attracted the attentions of Benoit Bard, a young laborer. He attacked her in the fields. Knowing the shame that would follow from the attack, "the clairvoyant" preferred death to rape and so offered a fierce resistance. Bard eventually knocked her unconscious and then raped her. "The brutal villager satisfied his ferocious passion."[31] She denounced him and he was condemned to hang by the senechausée of Riom; the verdict was upheld on appeal on April 19, 1780. That his sentence was carried out suggests that harsher penalties were given to poorer criminals.[32]

Yet Chevalier's fate was more typical. Bard and Aubert were casual laborers, rural wanderers not connected to family and neighborhood the way even the petite bourgeois Chevalier was, implying a class bias behind verdicts. The edict of 1730 stating that a rapist had to marry his victim or face capital punishment was seldom put into practice because it was believed that too many young couples wanting to marry without their parents' consent would stage a rape in order to circumvent parental authority. In James Farr's view this results in a virtual decriminalization of rape. He interprets the substitution of monetary restitution for corporal punishment, as well as the shift in the burden of litigation away from public prosecutors to private parties, to mean that authorities increasingly blamed the woman as well as the man.[33] No such blame was attributed to these victims, marks of their violent resistance clearing any suspicion of complicity.

But other women were blamed, either implicitly or explicitly. Indeed, in the case of Jeanne Ribes, a textile worker is blamed for "indiscretion," perhaps because she allowed herself to be alone in a community grain mill where the rape took place. The fact that she herself never reported the rape, and that there was no outraged father to avenge her, suggests that urban working women were vulnerable precisely to the degree that their movements precluded a reputation for virtue: they were public women unlike the rural shepherdess or domestic petite bourgeoise. What the misguided public accuses Ribes of is the murder of her newborn; otherwise, no one would have ever known about the rape. As a woman "on her own," Ribes was a prototypical alleged infanticide, as described by Olwen Hufton: "Aged between 20 and 30, engaged either as a servant, an employee in the textile trade (dentellière, fileuse, tricoteuse), a couturière, or as a casual laborer (a member of the great crowd of blanchisseuses and street traders), she was emphatically a woman on her own. . . ."[34] In the *Causes célèbres,* lawyers and editors also emphasized such women's motherlessness in order to further move judges and readers: the motherless child becomes the childless mother. The woman "on her own" was always depicted in these middle-class narratives as passive, vulnerable, and thereby easily victimized. Only the paternalistic compassion of the men who represented her could save her from facing dishonor or death. In all cases of alleged infanticide in the *Causes célèbres,* the accused are acquitted, thus demonstrating the degree to which even poor women, even those whose rapes are considered unremarkable, benefitted from the liberatory moment opened by defense strategies that challenged the power of tyrannical men and a misguided public opinion to ruin a woman's life.[35]

At the age of twenty, Jeanne Ribes, a textile worker, was raped by Thomas Barrau while at the community grain mill in Limoux in 1781. "Honest and religious," Ribes apparently knew nothing about her body; she did not realize that the rape resulted in her pregnancy. She attributed her missed menstrual cycles to a chill she had caught in a wine cellar. Neighbors and doctors prescribed a plethora of cures targeted to stimulate menstruation. Totally ignorant of the rape and cognizant of Ribes' blameless reputation, no one suspected that she might be pregnant. However, rumors began to spread when none of the traditional cures worked. Women in the community insulted Ribes' honor, suggesting that she had conceived illegitimately. They turned against her after her own mother had died, and the trope of the motherless child who becomes the childless mother enhances Des Essarts' depiction of Jeanne's vulnerability. "While Jeanne Ribes paid her last respects to the author of her days, evil was unleased against her. Some women who had witnessed the illness of her mother permitted themselves wicked thoughts."[36] Even her own brother heeded public opinion and urged Ribes to admit to the pregnancy and register it with the magistrates. She refused to acquiesce to what seemed to her a fantastical suggestion, so her brother evicted her from his house.

Ribes, recalling the rape, wondered if her missed periods could in fact be linked to the assault. Her defense emphasized her naiveté, alleging that she was ignorant of her body's functions. In this state of stupefaction she went into labor. Her brother permitted her to return to his home, and it was his neighbor, the widow Labatut, who first came to Jeanne's aid. Once Jeanne's pains had subsided, Labatut left her, still not realizing that Ribes was about to deliver. Her suffering resumed, and this time it was her sister-in-law who attended her. The suffering was so fierce that she thought Jeanne was dying. She ran to recall Labatut, leaving Jeanne alone. During this time, Ribes delivered an allegedly stillborn child. Panicked, her first thought was to dispose of the corpse, but before she could do so, her sister returned. At this point, she was forced to recount the rape.

During the night, the two women buried the corpse in the appropriate place, and Des Essarts suggests that neighbors spied on the whole episode. The child was consequently exhumed the next morning and the corpse was paraded about town as the people called out for Ribes' execution. An autopsy was performed to determine whether or not the child had been stillborn. The criminal assessor submerged a piece of the child's lung in water to determine if air had ever entered the body. The results were negative; the child had been born dead. However, neither the criminal assessor nor the crowd was satisfied, and Ribes was subjected to an "indecent" examination. After all, "it is necessary that there be a guilty party; and the public, nearly always an unjust judge when it heeds the stirrings of its natural impatience, determines itself to find one."[37] The impatient public, therefore, constructed here as irrational, is not a tribunal to be trusted. But Jeanne was then thrown into a prison cell to await sentencing. After two days of solitary confinement, she was condemned to death.

Fortunately for Ribes, Barère de Vieuzac, defender of Catherine Noailles and later regicide, appealed to the court on Ribes' behalf. In an emotionally charged summation, he persuaded the parlement to overturn the lower court's decision and to free his client. In his summation, Barère spoke out on Ribes' behalf, with all the sentimental drama of a *litterateur:*

> Would that she could appear before you surmounting the weakness and timidity of her sex, to seize the power of unhappy innocence and this courage that leads to truth! She would say: Oh my judges, why do you not protect the name 'mother' in your hearts? Have I not lived a prudent life, have I not maintained pure morals for twenty years to become in an instant an unnatural mother? Is it by murdering her baby that a mother begins her career? Do not slander nature. Oh, what witnesses saw me strangle it? What eyes saw my sacrilegious hand raised against an innocent victim? What ears heard its cries? Do you presume that in concealing its death I destroyed it? Oh, if you must presume, is this not in my favor? You insist that I have killed a baby, the most interesting being in nature! You believe that a mother could destroy pitilessly that which she loves most in the world![38]

To even imagine that a mother could murder her baby was to slander nature, esteemed here as the highest tribunal; if judges, appealed to as father-magistrates charged with protecting innocence, searched their hearts, they would find nature's inscription of the eternal mother. But just in case doubt lingered, Barère reminded the judges that there were no witnesses, adding the natural law defense to that based on maternal instinct. Because this tragedy left Ribes vulnerable to passion, her fear of dishonor causing temporary insanity, her lawyer emphasizes not the primacy of her reason but of her instinct, and therefore of her innocence.

Des Essarts also emphasized Ribes' maternal instinct in his chronicle. He reported how she was lifted out of her misery and misfortune during the brief moment just after giving birth. "In spite of her weakness, nearly dead, covered with blood, torn up with grief, she rose from her bed: maternal love gave her strength. Curious mother, she wanted to see her baby. . . . But what horror!"[39] In other words, nature triumphed over passion and her shame was eclipsed by motherly bliss. But her hopes of motherhood were dashed when she discovered the dead infant, and in the summation Barère indicated that at this moment Ribes' thoughts returned to her own deceased mother when no one else would understand.

Apropos of Ribes' behavior, Des Essarts lists her attributes as "innocence, feebleness, an intact reputation, an irreproachable conduct."[40] At first glance, then, the only inappropriate behavior in this case was that committed by Barrau, the rapist. But neither he nor the rape is brought to the attention of the authorities. Even Barère refrains from mentioning the rape. In fact, he focused on her failure to register her pregnancy, his silence implying that she was somehow responsible for her rape. Continuing the speech he made on her behalf, he has Ribes beg her deceased mother's forgiveness: "[Y]ou will forgive an involuntary error in order to comfort your unfortunate daughter."[41] The illicit behavior which led to her pregnancy made her guilty of an "involuntary error," but not of murder. Her motherlessness was intended to evoke as much pity as her childlessness, and her contrition reinforced how much she was at the judges' mercy.

Though the man commits the first crime against a woman, it is "opinion" that ruins her reputation, with its power to confer honor or shame. Again, it is clear that the crime itself is not enough to dishonor a woman; only public knowledge of the crime, inevitable once a baby enters the picture, leads inexorably to dishonor, and not just for the mother of the child but for the child itself. In another case, Lawyer Veillard de Boismartin summed this up well:

> [A mother] already foresees in the future the shame and dishonor which awaits the unfortunate fruit of her mistake, and leaves for his mother no other hope than a miserable life. What will become of her? What part to take in this sad crisis? Does she call upon the help of strangers? But her error does not permit this; and when she can do it, what will the Public say who has up until now been ignorant of her pregnancy? Does she expose herself to the nasty chatter of the people, who can never distinguish error from crime?[42]

Learned men sought to wrest justice away from the "nasty chatter of the people," and sometimes from the lower courts whose verdicts were too prone to error, too beholden to the misguided "people." The impact of Enlightenment calls for reform can especially be seen in infanticide trials in which lawyers appealed to magistrates on the double grounds of natural law and maternal instinct. Women like those considered here benefitted from these reforms, on the one-hand—they escaped capital punishment. On the other, the construction of women's nature by middle-class men rendered anachronistic, if not silent, those voices of townswomen who alleged the murderous intent and monstrous capabilities of women whom they knew to be more than passive victims and selfless mothers.

Yet Ribes was a passive victim of male violence. What of the women whose pregnancies were not involuntary, those who were seduced like Martin or in love like Duel, or those whose extramarital sexual activity like Alliot led to pregnancy? Their defense insisted on their virtue, sometimes demonizing the man who betrayed them, sometimes praising the natural inclinations which led the young to form families outside the rigors of the law. But what if their infants had been stillborn? What if they had in fact murdered them? The next few brief cases illustrate the range of women whose transgressive behaviors did not garner hostile representations or unfavorable verdicts, illustrating the degree to which "a certain emancipation of women" influenced the fate of even poor women.

In the mid-eighteenth century, Lawyer Robin defended his client against charges of infanticide by castigating both the man who wronged her in the first place and the society forced a victimized woman to face dishonor or death, to bear the shame of an illegitimate child or the guilt of causing her infant to die. With the romanticization of motherly love, the possibility that a woman could murder her offspring could only be explained by temporary insanity, or unchecked passion resulting from the dread of dishonor; in either case she should be acquitted, so went the standard defense. Thus, all women, even those suspected of the most "unnatural" of crimes found favorable hearings in the courtrooms and in the popular press.

Indeed, the next case was among the first Des Essarts published. In the early part of the eighteenth century, Demoiselle Chanas married Monsieur Loreau and bore him a daughter. Decades later, she moved in with her daughter after her husband's untimely death. Desiring to end her widowhood, she became involved with a young man who seduced and abandoned her. This "monster" accepted no responsibility for the pregnancy and Chanas was left alone, placed between dishonor and death. Seeking a third option, she apparently hoped to conceal the affair and declined to register her pregnancy. Chanas gave birth secretly and alone, and the baby was indeed found dead the next morning. The public prosecutor charged her with infanticide and within hours she was condemned to die. Robin appealed her case to the parlement of Grenoble, pleading:

> The day will undoubtedly come . . . when the cry of the nation's enlightened men will be raised up against the opinion which seems to place a girl between dishonor and death, and bring this important issue before the attention of the legislator.

> A woman has made a mistake: she counted on the faith of a man who should legitimize a premature engagement and protect her from the suspicion that she is concealing a pregnancy: how many such monsters, after having sacrificed victims to their passion, finish by betraying them?[43]

With his moving rhetoric, he was able to obtain a commutation of her sentence to ten-years' banishment and a fine of ten livres. Was she guilty of infanticide, then? Of merely breaking the law requiring registration? Did the higher court lessen her sentence because of extenuating circumstances, because she acted out of passion? But did such motivation render her an inhuman "monster" who must be purged from the community, or a victim herself of untenable choices?

Marie Maire was another vulnerable woman on her own. She was, as a seamstress, "exposed to all types of seduction" as her work required her to go from house to house. Des Essarts points out that she was virtuous and succumbed to these seductions only twice, his choice of verb questioning her degree of agency, but note that she is not a rape victim, as was Ribes. Note, too, that like Rousseau's Julie she is still described as virtuous despite transgressive sexual behavior. But in July, 1785, the townswomen of Saint-Jean de Lone accused her of infanticide and subjected her to an impromptu physical examination; a local doctor confirmed their diagnosis. Maire then admitted to a miscarriage in the fourth or fifth month of pregnancy and to having buried the corpse outside her window. Could infanticide be proven? No corpse could be found and so a medical expert from Dijon was summoned to testify. He claimed that what she expelled may not have been a baby. Her lawyer then urged the judges to give her the benefit of the doubt, especially since "public opinion always exaggerates. . . . Public clamor rarely leads to truth."[44] Maire was acquitted by the Parlement of Dijon on February 13, 1786.

Even a woman still more fallen than Maire or Chanas was treated sympathetically. Marguerite Maubach was a woman of questionable virtue, "she had had adventures and successive moments of weakness, but her heart was more impressionable than vile, more tender than interested, and one can accuse her of no other vice than the need to be loved."[45] Lacking interestedness, unlike all of the men featured in the trials considered thus far, the woman on her own was the epitome of vulnerability, vulnerable to male predators, but especially to public opinion, and therefore most in need of the enlightened protection of father-magistrates who recognized true virtue and were immune to public clamor.

Yet these father-magistrates, having no self-interest in the cases of infanticide they heard and seeing no general interest at stake, did not call for the punishment of the men who abused these women in the first place, and did not, as Merrick pointed out above, articulate "a vindication of the rights of woman as such." Even Des Essarts does not explicitly offer a vindication. The only proposal to assist unmarried pregnant women he applauded was the building of more foundling hospitals. To a case similar to Ribes', he appended a pamphlet on infanticide published in the *Mercure* in 1782.[46] This anonymous author depicted a woman's plight in moving terms, and explained why, out of desperation, a woman would want to do away with unwanted offspring. Des Essarts enthusiastically welcomed the pamphleteer's suggestions on the ways to prevent infanticide: "We are very far from adopting all the ideas for reform which this brochure contains; but it is surely the work of a sensitive soul and eloquent pen; and we take sweet pleasure in paying the author this deserved tribute of praises."[47]

In short, the author of the pamphlet believed that there would always be unwanted children because women were bound to end up the victims of cruel seducers and of their own desires. And as long as society continued to scorn women who mothered illegitimate children, even, as has been seen, if the pregnancy were the result of rape, women would rather eliminate the evidence and maintain a reputation for honor. Given that the pamphleteer believed that none of these facts of life could be changed, the only way to save the lives of these unwanted babes was to build more foundling hospitals.[48] The author argued that every town should have at least one and that confidentiality must be guaranteed. "What girl could be so cruel as to put to death the child to whom she has just given life if she is aware of a repository where she could put it with confidence and without dishonor?"[49] Thus some commentators acknowledged that despite maternal instinct, some women might "be so cruel" as to turn against nature and in a moment of insanity murder her own offspring.

But not the women featured in the *Causes célèbres*. Women were never found guilty of infanticide because either there was no proof (as in the case of Maire) or because their emotional state rendered them temporarily insane (as in the case of Chanas). It was always a misguided public opinion, especially the "clamor" of women, which created a *causes célèbre* where none would otherwise exist. Yet all of these women did in fact bury corpses under mysterious circumstances, hoping thereby to conceal something. But what? Indeed, infanticide was but one of several strategies of concealment. Contraception and abortion were also used to maintain appearances, and for wealthy families "lettres de cachet" might prevent an individual's behavior from dishonoring the whole family. Aristocrats like the de Rois family especially preferred this approach to correction, and in some cases of alleged adultery, wives would be thusly imprisoned. Often, however, circumstances like pregnancy could not be concealed from the public, especially among the people.

Despite his reticence to endorse the verdicts of the public or the people, and though he sympathized with the plight of the virtuous woman in every case considered here, Des Essarts continued to maintain that "[women's] civil existence depends, in some way, on their reputations; every woman who lacks honor is degraded and excluded from the company of respectable people."[50] He thus implies women's motives for concealment and dissimulation. Stated more as a fact than as a prescription, he would argue that at the very least women be redeemed in law if not in opinion. This echoes Rousseau's famous dictum: "A man has no one but himself to consider, and so long as he does right he may defy public opinion; but when a woman does right, her task is only half finished, and what people think of her matters as much as what she really is . . . ; among men, opinion is the tomb of virtue; among women it is the throne."[51] Though Des Essarts maintained an ambivalence about the hegemony of opinion, both formulations reinforce the dominance of opinion in constructing women's honor, even as they acknowledge that opinion can be wrong. Thus the narrative of liberation is undercut by a counternarrative that maintains women's subservience to their constructed reputations.

Dissimulation, antithetical to transparent virtue, was possible for some women who were increasingly able to absent themselves from the public gaze as they retreated into the private sphere or, if they were women of the people, to be freed from the crueller consequences of illicit sexual activity, whether voluntary or not. But in the end the defiant individualism of the Rousseauian "homo clausus" was all but impossible for women. Men could risk dishonor because what mattered to Rousseau—and later to Republicans of Virtue—was not reputation, but innate and inalterable virtue, a "virtue" whose masculine content is implicit in its etymology when women are admonished to cultivate "appearance" over essence. And although many lawyers came close to advocating a similar independence from public opinion for women, republicans following Rousseau would seldom go that far: women were always to be trapped by the panoptic gaze of a society whose mandates for gendered behavior perpetuated, or even exacerbated, traditional strictures on sexual practice.

Republicans following Rousseau inherited the tension between narrative and counternarrative that characterize the "certain emancipation of women" underway in the 1780s. While endorsing, even reifying, sentimental maternity, this time in the context of the national good, women's range of private behaviors in the context of the republican family expanded as stigmas against illegitimacy, adoption, and divorce were relaxed and as natural, fecundity was sanctioned in a greater variety of unions than ever before. Thus, women like Beaumont, Ribes, Chanas, Maire, and Maubach would not need foundling hospitals or unmarked graves to dispose of the fruits of their shame, for their shame would be mitigated and they would be encouraged to marry because everything could be started anew.[52] At the same time, women's public behaviors, especially when they did not rest on sentimental maternity and natural fecundity, were increasingly proscribed. The collision between these two mandates is illustrated by the fate of the revolutionary heroine Manon Roland whose case was anthologized by Des Essarts in 1797. By explicating his representation of Roland, we glimpse the end of the liberatory moment made possible by the very representations he peddled so effectively, which contributed to "a certain emancipation of women."

Conclusion:
The Republic of Virtue

> It seems, in effect, that miserly nature only rarely produces souls strong and passionate enough for virtue. . . The ascendancy of a great character of this type is that much more powerful because nature has put in the heart of man an irresistible attraction for a beautiful and virtuous woman, and because, if chance places this woman at the center of attention and the greatest interests, it depends on her to direct public opinion towards crime or virtue. This was the situation of citizen Roland.[1]

DES ESSARTS RECOGNIZED THE POTENCY OF VIRTUE COMBINED WITH passion, beauty, and access to power. Sympathetic with Roland's politics, he nevertheless evinced a nervousness about her power in his acknowledgment that she controlled the ever-volatile public opinion.

As seen in the previous chapter, Des Essarts noted that the verdicts of public opinion could be cruel if not wrong. Because it conferred honor or shame, it refused to liberate women even when the court's verdicts did. Because it could be led astray by the hysterical people or, in revolutionary times, by demagogues, Des Essarts persisted in his skepticism about its power. But he did acknowledge throughout the *Causes célèbres* that an enlightened form of public opinion could function as a tribune above laws and customs still beholden to the prejudices of rank and status. Keith Baker has described its evolution: "'Public opinion' emerged in eighteenth-century political discourse as an abstract category, invoked by actors in a new kind of politics to secure the legitimacy of claims that could no longer be made binding in the terms (and within the traditional institutional circuit) of an absolutist political order."[2] Defined by Rousseau and others, it was an appropriate antecedent to the general will. In March 1789, for example, lawyer Desherbier prosecuted an "innocent" man wrongly charged by a widow with her husband's murder. When the lawyer for the defense, Godard, reminded the courts of the host of innocents condemned by public opinion, urging them to share with him "some reflections on the quite common and dangerous errors of so-called public opinion," Desherbier retorted with a defense of "public opinion, which is the sum total of the pure sentiments of each individual in society, and which will be eternally and appropriately named the universal conscience. . . . it is founded on the movements of a compassionate humanity, and the natural horror of crime; attempt to guide it, if you can, but do not slander it."[3] Universal conscience, pure sentiments, general will?

Throughout the Revolution, as well as in cases like Desherbier's, competing parties sought to control public opinion and to justify their actions by appealing to it. Those who believed themselves capable of transcending self-interest claimed to represent it. Even Roland made this claim in her trial, distinguishing between the verdicts of the people and a universal virtue, as had Des Essarts. And while he praised her virtue, he wondered whether or not she should control public opinion when in fact she already possessed the formidable power of attractiveness. This ultimate form of control over men, desire, evoked fear and, notoriously, was used to justify women's confinement to the private sphere. Yet Roland was a public figure *and* an exemplar of virtue. Des Essarts' account of her life and death traces the interaction between narrative and counter-narrative at the moment when women's opportunities were foreclosed, brutally in Roland's case. She was guillotined in 1793 for allegedly participating in a Girondist conspiracy.[4]

Des Essarts used his account of her case to participate in the polemics of the Year VII. He was a moderate throughout the Revolution and probably a Girondist sympathizer. When the Bastille fell, he engaged in the fighting and was promptly made a major in the Passy section of the National Guard. Shortly afterward, he left the National Guard to become an elector in Paris. This appointment earned him the envy of many, and libels were printed and distributed against him which aimed to discredit him, a career not unlike that of Roland and her husband. Des Essarts' detractors accused him of being an "apologist for despotism," a spy for the police. In his published "Réponse à ses calomniateurs" (Paris, date unknown), he answered that the past was behind him: "I believed that in a moment of revolution, when the country is in danger, every good citizen must sacrifice himself to save it"—words Roland would also speak in due time. When the revolution moved into its more radical phases, his period of self-sacrifice ended and Des Essarts dropped out of political life. When it was finally safe to do so, he used this position of safety denied to Roland and denounced Robespierre as "the most execrable of tyrants, the vilest of scoundrels, the most hypocritical, the most cowardly, the most ferocious of monsters."[5]

Deploying the trope of monstrosity to convey the unnatural and inhuman disposition of the murderer and the tyrant (as he had done in those *causes célèbre* featuring violent crimes), Des Essarts explained her execution at the hands of the Jacobins whom he described as "those monsters [who] knew that this courageous woman recognized them as ferocious beasts." He expressed outrage against the Jacobin monsters who, finding their just desserts on the scaffold, compared themselves to Roland: how dare they! He lamented his obligation to recount this horrible story at all, but he believed the chronicle of these travesties to be "the best means for preventing the return of similar atrocities." He wanted "to engrave them in history, and attach to the memory of the authors [of these crimes] the seal of infamy."[6] Like the didacticism of the *Causes célèbres,* his later writings continued to offer "so many lessons" for individuals of both sexes.

What lessons could be derived from the life story of Manon Roland? Her trajectory towards virtue began in early childhood. Des Essarts credited nature and a doting father for endowing the girl with intelligence and virtue. An engraver's daughter, she was a member of the petite bourgeoisie, an honest and hard-working social class, a group which he tended to favor in the *Causes célèbres.* The daughter of a pious and modest woman, Manon learned domesticity from an excellent role model. He described her mother: "[R]easonable and good by nature, virtue appeared to cost her nothing. She knew how to render her daughter sweet and gentle like herself. Wise and calm, tender without being passionate, her soul pure and tranquil . . . ,"[7] she possessed quintessential virtue and would likely have resisted the fervor which drove her daughter into politics when the Revolution broke out.

Such piety was shared by Manon only into early adolescence, though the friendship she made during her convent education with a Sister Agatha lasted her whole life and is a testament to the kind of personal piety she maintained even after rejecting the superstitious church. Familiarity with the works of the ancients as well as Enlightenment philosophy eventually tempered Manon's religion and fostered republicanism. He mentions that she took Plutarch to church in the guise of *Semaine-sainte.* He dwells at some length on her devotion to her mother, the love of whom was "the only sentiment which animated her soul." When her mother died, even philosophy could not console her and her tender and "sensible" heart seemed forever broken.

But then she discovered Rousseau's *La Nouvelle Heloïse* and this changed her life. All the better for a Republican mother, such as she was destined to be. She married Jean-Marie Roland de la Platière that year, 1775, and shortly thereafter gave birth to their daughter Eudora. In her domesticity, she read Rousseau's *Emile* and apparently became a disciple, breast-feeding her daughter, participating fully in the cult of *sensibilité* and Republicanism that typified Rousseau's followers of both genders.

Yet the world of the private sphere was not enough for this wife of an important man destined for a political career in tumultuous times. Her philosophical mind and her talent for rhetoric made her a natural choice for her husband's secretary when he was appointed Minister of the Interior in 1792. She was known to have written many of his important letters and speeches. She also hosted political gatherings in her home. When the Girondins were purged from the Convention (the central governing body from 1792–95), she was among a loose group of individuals variously accused of royalism, war-mongering, federalism, and, notably, self-interest in a trial in 1793 which resulted in her execution. Barère de Vieuzac, who had made his career defending wronged women like Catherine Noailles and Jeanne Ribes against aristocrats, patriarchs, and public opinion, was by 1793 a hard-line radical who accused the Girondins, including Roland, of "carefully crafted plots of moderatism" in his speech enumerating their crimes.[8]

Roland's "crime" was pure virtue combined with an audacity which ultimately compromised her. Thus, for Des Essarts, she had achieved the ideal: having constructed a modern identity capable of autonomous action based on moral judgement that was rooted in domesticity. Ironically, revolutionary developments gave her the opportunity to manifest her virtue even as they propelled her into public action. In letters and other public pronouncements, often published under her husband's name, she had "torn away the masks which hid these terrifying assassins of September second and third."[9] She even called for a proscription against the radicals, or "Mountain," after their complicity in prison massacres which took the lives of some 1,200 in Parisian jails in early September 1792. Appropriately maternal, she was also capable of the self-sacrifice required by her country when in turmoil. Des Essarts' comments on her stay in prison reveal that through it all she retained her Republican motherliness, giving comfort to those prisoners less stalwart than she, even allowing her companion at the scaffold to go before her so that he would be spared the horror of seeing her perish. Through her acts of self-sacrifice she constituted her self-determination. Moderate in her passions, she stood above the "fanatics" who Des Essarts decried for "peopl[ing] France with assassins."[10]

But this laudatory narrative does not stop there. In the interest of "objectivity," Des Essarts attached to the end of his account of her trial several excerpts from her diaries which show her in an "unflattering" light: "One finds therein some stains which disparage her, but these defects of the spirit and of an exalted sense of self are redeemed by great talents, and above all by virtue. We would not make these remarks if we respected the duties of the historian less. We have promised to be impartial in our judgments."[11] He had to find fault with her, implying that such an "exalted sense of self" was inappropriate to the domestic ideal she represented. At the same time, the very virtue which emanated from that domesticity redeemed her, much as it had redeemed all of the women whose transgressions were narrated throughout the *Causes célèbres*.

In her diary, she described the role she played in her husband's political career. "[Roland] often concluded by persuading himself that it had been good luck when he had written such passages [which really came from] my pen." Manon's skills were not limited to letter writing; she was clever enough to convince her husband that her talents were really his, that his accomplishments were his own. Yet she knew the truth: "If it were a question of expressing great or strong truths, I would put my whole soul into it; it was quite plain that his expression would be better for the spirited efforts of his secretary."[12] Her audacity intensified as she wrote about her approaching end.

Though Des Essarts himself had likened her to a "great man" in the degree of courage she possessed, he believed he had demonstrated her arrogance by featuring her own words at the scaffold when she said she was proud "to share the fate of the great men whom you have murdered." At the foot of the guillotine, the blood lust of the people would find its ultimate satiation. When she approached the scaffold, the people shouted: "Down with traitors!" To this she replied, "I will go there. I will be there in a moment, but those who sent me here will not be long in following me. I come here innocent; they will come as criminals, and you who applaud today will applaud then."[13] Again it is clear that the people were indiscriminant; they turned against those whom they formerly adored, fooled by demagogues. For this, Des Essarts, as well as Roland herself, condemned them.

Further, Roland described herself as the ideal citizen, free from the taint of self-interest, and in that, perfectly virtuous: "I loved my country. I was an enthusiast for liberty; I knew of no other interest or passion which could compete with those." If the ability to place the general interest over the particular is essential to the possession of modern citizenship, then Roland surely demonstrates a "certain emancipation of women." But revolutionary circumstances made her appear a conspicuous exception and she knew that her singularity would lead to her death. "This [my condemnation] has proven to me even more the scarcity of my type in this country, [a fact] which inspires an elevated idea of myself. It is not the spirit which is lacking—it is everywhere in the streets—but the justice of judgement and the force of character."[14]

As evidenced by the constellation of other notable women executed that Fall (Olympe de Gouges, Charlotte Corday, and Marie Antoinette), Jacobins did not see Manon as that different from either the powerful aristocratic women whom they believed ruled (and ruined) Old Regime France or the celibate "harpies" jeopardizing the new. Jacobins used her case, as well as those of other revolutionary women, to justify policies excluding women from public life.[15] Articulating a counternarrative, they constructed Roland as outside Nature. The "Moniteur Universel" invariably represented all of these women, regardless of their "crimes," as "unnatural," "monstrous," or "unsexed." Roland in particular was said to have "sacrificed Nature by trying to raise herself above it."[16] Virtuous and powerful, this beautiful woman active in the public sphere was either described as the pinnacle of virtue or else monstrous. In her singular example, narrative and counternarrative resulted in her apotheosis as well as her destruction.

A Certain Emancipation of Women interrogates narrative and counternarrative in the eighteenth-century French discourse on women's behavior. As seen in the case of Roland, who was both representation of virtue and historical actor, tensions implicit in the *Causes célèbres* reached an impasse in 1793. On the one hand, sentimental constructions of tormented virtue enabled lawyers and editors to secure a measure of independence for women from self-interested fathers and husbands. Winning their cases, women benefited from a liberatory moment that facilitated the evolution of modern gendered identities: women defined themselves and were recognized as reasonable beings, capable of autonomous action and sound judgment. This moment was characteristically late Enlightenment: criticisms of male power were couched in terms of natural law, secular individualism, and *sensibilité*. On the other hand, the space created by such liberation led inexorably to a greater presence of women in all aspects of public life. In the context of the tumultuous events of the early 1790s, reactionaries decried women's claims to, and exercise of, citizenship just at the moment when women like Roland (and de Gouges and even Corday, to name only the most famous) seized public space for themselves.

Contestation over the meaning of citizenship, predicated on an individualism simultaneously requires the erasure and the recognition of difference, is inevitable, especially when it is a question of "female citizenship." This study of the *Causes célèbres* thus leads to at least two potentially mutually exclusive conclusions. Explicating the discourse on virtue in late-eighteenth-century France, a "certain emancipation of women" was achieved by lawyers and editors who "liberated" virtuous women from self-interested men. This emancipation was, however, undercut by that very discourse on virtue which emphasized women's difference. At the level of representation, this difference has been seen as confining. At the level of lived experience, real women's lives were more complicated than ideologies of domesticity suggest, and real women were more actively engaged in the construction of their identities, using such representations to achieve their own emancipation.

The role played by the best-selling *Causes célèbres* in this process is the focal point of the present work, for it uniquely bridges the gap between representation and lived experience, enabling an analysis of the degree to which one influenced the other. A study of it in the context of the late Enlightenment and early Revolution makes clear that a shift in mentality had taken place which would not be eradicated by late revolutionary legislative decrees and the Napoleonic Code. Perhaps the moment of foreclosure reaching its apex in the late 1790s was just a moment; perhaps developments in the period from the 1770s to the Republic of Virtue proved more durable.

By examining the issues which embroiled women in *causes célèbres*—seductions, separations, rape, inheritance disputes, infanticide, adultery, and murder—it becomes clear that norms for women's behavior expanded and greater liberation was granted to a greater number. The stories told in the *Causes célèbres* are veritable enactments of a social contract wherein individuals enter into families through birth and marriage, and then into civil society, by manifesting virtue, if not always by following specific rites. Only in a *causes célèbre* something has gone awry: a failed citizen is brought before the courts to stand judgment. In this way the *Causes célèbres* is ironic, for in literally hundreds of cases, individuals—especially interested and powerful men—fail to live up to the roles constructed for them. But that failure, when brought to the attention of the courts, and eventually hundreds of readers, enabled revisions in the family romance with radical, and long-lasting, consequences.

The *Causes célèbres* contributed to such revisions by providing a broad reading audience with representations of honorable and dishonorable behavior. Because of their comprehensive scope and popularity, and because of the numbers of revolutionary personnel who either participated in or were influenced by them, they are practically unrivaled as a source for tracing the impact of discourses on virtue prevalent in the late Enlightenment. Moreover, because women continued to be a forceful presence in the *literary* public sphere (as Habermas pointed out), texts like those included in the *Causes célèbres* are especially central to understanding the process by which both normative and subversive forms of individual subjectivity as well as modern citizenship were constituted.

While virtuous women were encouraged to act independently, and to speak their truth, as seen in the case of Manon Roland, such independence and the arrogance it fostered could lead to tragic death. During the Revolution, honor retained its association with appropriate sexual behavior, only now appropriate behavior was judged by the mandates of citizenship. And virtue was deemed superior to honor: at first because it was divorced from family association and was inherent in the individual—and thereby less tentative than honor; later, because of its masculine content—which limited its manifestation to the public sphere. Women like Roland were deemed virtuous, but they were not supposed to take literally its mandate to emulate masculine power. Roland's inappropriate behavior rested not on the use of her literal body—in this she had conformed to the ideal—but in her claim to possess a political body as well.

But even for the goals of a gender-specific citizenship to be achieved—separate spheres, republican motherhood, the cult of domesticity—traditional forms of patriarchal authority would be questioned, revised, in some instances defeated. Concepts of individual personhood and citizenship were redefined, as were concomitant definitions of honor and virtue. For just as the image of the domestic angel of the house began to permeate prescriptive literature, and her likeness can be glimpsed in the women whose cases we have considered, so too was paternal authority undermined by the rhetoric of lawyers in the Noailles, Martin, Duel, and Alliot cases (chapters two and three); the authority of husbands was similarly undermined in all of the suits for separation featured in chapter three; virtuous women were deemed to be the authorities of their own experiences of rape, sex, or childbirth in the Martin, Alliot, Beaumont, and Ribes cases (chapters two, three, and four); and women's independence was fostered by the admonition to resist violent or criminal men and even to defy public opinion in nearly every case. A composite construction of the new female citizen would include Beaumont and Noailles, surely, but also Alliot and Dames D. and L. In fact, representations of female citizenship are discernable in all of the *Causes célèbres.* During the Republic of Virtue such women would find in revolutionary legislation more opportunities for domestic bliss, but no actual political empowerment.

In short, in the years before the French Revolution, women who would be citizens were "liberated" from more traditional forms of authority in order to become directly responsible for their actions to the state, and in the process constructed their identities as reasonable individuals capable of virtue and moral autonomy. Resistance to "interested" or corrupt husbands and fathers, or to a misguided public opinion, was justified, in some cases mandated, and can only be called "a certain emancipation." Though its trajectory in France was uneven, beset by periods of advance and retreat, this certain emancipation was pushed through by determined feminists throughout the nineteenth and twentieth centuries. Thus, the process unfolding in the 1770s and 1780s, to which the *Causes célèbres* was essential, contributed to an emancipation of women that was "certain" in the sense of tentative and "certain" in the sense of absolute.

Notes

Introduction

1. Nicolas Toussaint Le Moyne Des Essarts, *Causes célèbres, curieuses et intéressantes de toutes les cours souveraines du Royaume avec les jugements qui les ont decidées* 6, case 40 (1773),179–80.

2. This formulation of the argument bears the influence of two recent works: Carla Hesse, *The* Other *Enlightenment: How French Women Became Modern* (Princeton University Press, 2001), xiv, and Marisa Linton, *The Politics of Virtue in Enlightenment France* (New York: Palgrave, 2001), 4.

3. See Tracey Rizzo, "'A Lascivious Climate': Representations of Colonial Subjectivity in the *Causes célèbres* of Eighteenth-century France," *Journal of Caribbean History* 2000, 34 (1–2): 157–77.

4. See note 11, below.

5. Alain Lottin and G. Savelon, "Les Divorcés" in *La désunion du couple sous l'Ancien Regime: l'Example du nord,* ed. Alain Lottin (Paris: Editions universitaires, 1975), 114.

6. Joan Landes' work is at the forefront of this scholarship. See *Visualizing the Nation: Gender, Representation, and Revolution in Eighteenth-century France* (Ithaca: Cornell University Press, 2001) and *Women and the Public Sphere in the Age of the French Revolution* (Ithaca : Cornell University Press, 1988).

On the role of virtue in the evolution of French nationalism more generally, see David Bell, *The Cult of the Nation in France* (Cambridge: Harvard University Press, 2001). On representations of female virtue, see Mary L. Jacobus, "Incorruptible Milk: Breast-feeding and the French Revolution," in *Rebel Daughters: Women and the French Revolution,* eds. Sara E. Melzer and Leslie W. Rabine (New York: Oxford University Press, 1992). On Marianne, see Lynn Hunt, *Politics, Culture and Class in the French Revolution* (Berkeley: University of California Press, 1984).

7. Jeffrey Merrick, "Domestic Politics: Divorce and Despotism in Eighteenth-Century France," in *The Past as Prologue: ASECS at Twenty-Five,* ed. Carla Hay and Sydney Conger (New York: AMS press, 1995), 13; and Nadine Berenguier, "Victorious Victims: Women and Publicity in *Memoires Judiciaires,*" in *Going Public: Women and Publishing in Early Modern France,* eds. Elizabeth C. Goldsmith and Dena Goodman (Ithaca: Cornell University Press, 1995), 78.

8. Joan Wallach Scott, *Only Paradoxes to Offer: French Feminists and the Rights of Man* (Cambridge: Harvard University Press, 1996), 3.

9. Hesse, xiv.

10. Yet the legacy of Jacobinism is also paradoxical. See note 20 below.

11. Linton, "Virtue Rewarded? Women and the Politics of Virtue in 18th-Century France. Part II," *Journal of History of European Ideas* 26 (2000), 55.

12. Des Essarts, "Emile et Sophie, ou les époux désunis," (Paris: Nyon, 1784).

13. Peter Brooks, *The Melodramatic Imagination* (New Haven: Yale University Press, 1976).

14. Jürgen Habermas, *The Structural Transformation of the Public Sphere*, trans. Thomas Burger (Cambridge: MIT Press, 1989), 56.

15. On the degree to which virtue and nobility became disassociated, even incompatible, in the eighteenth century, see Jay Smith, *The Culture of Merit* (Ann Arbor: University of Michigan Press, 1996), and John Shovlin, "Toward a Reinterpretation of Revolutionary Anti-nobilism: The Political Economy of Honor in the Old Regime," *Journal of Modern History* 72 1 (2000): 35–66.

16. *Causes célèbres* 68, case 177 (1780), 27.

17. *Causes célèbres* 97, case 308 (1782), 25.

18. Sarah Maza, "The Rose-Girl of Salency: Representations of Virtue in Prerevolutionary France," *Eighteenth-Century Studies* 22 (3), Spring 1989: 400.

19. Maza, *Private Lives and Public Affairs: The Causes célèbres of Prerevolutionary France* (Berkeley: University of California, 1993), 321.

20. Scott, 20.

21. Patrice Higonnet, *Goodness Beyond Virtue: Jacobins During the French Revolution* (Cambridge: Harvard University Press, 1998), 135, 94.

22. J. J. Rousseau, *Lettre à M. d'Alembert sur le thèatre* (Geneva: Droz, 1758; 1948) in *Politics and the Arts: Letter to M. d'Alembert on the Theatre*, trans. Alan Bloom, (Ithaca: Cornell University Press, 1960), 88. Quoted in Landes, *Women*, 85.

23. Rousseau, *Oeuvres complètes*, ed. Bernard Gagnebin and Marcel Raymond, vol. 4: "Emile" (Paris: Pléiade, 1969) 709–10, quoted in Carol Blum, *Rousseau and the Republic of Virtue* (Ithaca: Cornell University Press, 1986), 91.

24. *Causes célèbres* 101, case 327 (1783): 119–20.

25. Blum, *Rousseau and the Republic of Virtue*, 63.

26. Rousseau, *Oeuvres complètes*, vol. 4: "Emile," 258, quoted in Blum, 47.

27. Joan Landes, *Women*, 21.

28. Rousseau, *Oeuvres complètes*, vol. 3: "Ecrits politiques," 14–15, quoted in Blum, 41.

29. Rousseau, 966, quoted in Blum, 116.

30. *Causes célèbres* 134, case 485 (1785): 4.

31. *Causes célèbres* 102, case 328 (1783): 32–33.

32. *Procès fameux: Extraits de l'essai sur l'histoire générale des tribunaux des peuples*, 9 (Paris: 1786), 78.

33. Chantal Thomas, "Heroism in the Feminine: The Examples of Charlotte Corday and Madame Roland," *Eighteenth-Century Theory and Interpretation:* (Special Issue) 30, 1989: 69.

34. Des Essarts, *Procès Fameux jugés depuis la Révolution* vol. 11 (Paris: by the Author, An 7): 140.

Chapter 1. The *Causes Célèbres*

1. *Procès fameux:* 9, 73.
2. Ibid., 72.
3. Ibid., 78.
4. *Causes célèbres* 77, case 213 (1781): 176.
5. Anne C. Vila, *Enlightenment and Pathology* (Baltimore: Johns Hopkins University Press, 1998), 243.
6. *Procès fameux,* 78.
7. Hans Jürgen Lüsebrink, "Les répresentations sociales de la criminalité en France au XVIIIè siècle," diss., Ecole des Hautes Etudes en Sciences sociales, Paris, 1983, 177. Lüsebrink is the only other scholar to study Des Essarts' *Causes célèbres.*
8. Quoted in David Bell, *Lawyers and Citizens: The Making of a Political Elite in Old Regime France* (Oxford: Oxford University Press, 1994), 155.
9. *Causes célèbres* 106, case 344 (1783): 13–14.
10. *Causes célèbres* 90, case 277 (1782): 179.
11. Des Essarts, quoted in Isabelle Vissière, "Introduction," *Procès des Femmes au Temps des Philosophes* (Paris: des Femmes, 1985), 9, 10.
12. Des Essarts, "Discours préliminaire," in *Essai sur l'Histoire général des Tribunaux des peuples, tant anciens que modernes* (Paris, 1778), ii–iii.
13. Des Essarts, *Essai sur l'Histoire generale des tribunaux des peuples* (Paris: 1778), vol.1, 1.
14. Roger Chartier, "Urban Reading Practices, 1660–1780," *The Cultural Uses of Print in Early-Modern Europe,* trans. Lydia Cochrane (Princeton: Princeton University Press, 1987).
15. Des Essarts, *Proces fameux* (Paris: 1786), vol 1, advertisement (quoted in Lüsebrink, "Les répresentations," 137). Subscription costs could be prohibitively expensive at 18 livres per year for Paris and 24 elsewhere. Single issues could be purchased for 2 livres, 10 sols.
16. Lüsebrink, "Les répresentations," 138. Richer joined Des Essarts as co-editor in the last years of the journal's existence.
17. Lüsebrink, "Les répresentations," 139, and Lüsebrink, "Les crimes sexuelles dans les *Causes célèbres,*" *Dix-huitième siècle* 12 (1980): 153.
18. Lüsebrink, "Les répresentations," 188–89.
19. Lüsebrink, "Les répresentations," 177. Of fifteen leading journals studied by Lüsebrink, only two failed to mention the *Causes célèbres* during the entire duration of their publication. One of the fifteen, the juridically oriented *Gazette des Tribunaux,* reported on either Des Essarts' collection or that of his occasional collaborator, François Richer, twenty-seven times between 1774 and 1789, "generally very positive and often detailed." Of the combined thirty-nine reviews of Des Essarts' collection, thirty were positive, eight were neutral, and one was mixed.
20. Bell, *Lawyers and Citizens,* 164.
21. See Jeffrey Merrick, "Fathers and Kings: Patriarchalism and Absolutism in Eighteenth-Century French Politics," *Studies on Voltaire and the Eighteenth Century* 308 (1993): 281–303.
22. Darline Levy cited by Nadine Bérenguier in "Fiction dans les archives: Adultère et stratégies de défense dans deux mémoires judiciaires au XVIIIe siè-

cle," *Studies on Voltaire and the Eighteenth Century* 308 (1993): 269. Levy is referring to Simon-Henri Linguet, the best known of the new breed of lawyers. See also David Bell's discussion of Linguet in *Lawyers and Citizens.*

23. Blum, *Rousseau and the Republic of Virtue,* 181.

24. Alain Lottin, "Le couple et sa désagrégation,"149.

25. *Causes célèbres* 117, case 391 (1784): 207.

26. For all of the cases included in the present study, memoirs were available only for the Alliot case discussed in chapter three. For that case, there was no difference between Alliot's lawyer's memoirs and Des Essarts' version. These memoirs, along with other writings relevant to the case, are known as factums. Interested readers may consult Augustin Corda's *Catalogue des factums et d'autres documents judiciaires antérieurs à 1790,* 7 vols. (Paris: Plon, 1890–1905), which provides an alphabetical listing of factums held at the Bibliothèque Nationale.

27. Maurice Daumas, *L'Affaire D'Esclans: Les conflits familiaux au dix-huitième siècle* (Paris: Seuil, 1988), 12.

28. Maza, "Domestic Melodrama as Political Ideology: the Case of the Comte de Sanois," *American Historical Review* 94 (December 1989): 1253.

29. Bell, "Lawyers and Politics in Eighteenth-Century France," diss., Princeton: Princeton University Press, 1991, 80.

30. Lenard Berlanstein, *The Barristers of Toulouse in the Eighteenth Century (1740–1793)* (Baltimore: Johns Hopkins University Press, 1975), 5.

31. Entries for Des Essarts in France's national biographical encyclopedias do not give more specific details. David Garrioch notes that "Some 1,431 men qualified as 'avocats au Parlement' in the 30 years between 1760 and 1790" in *Neighbourhood and Community in Paris, 1740–1790* (Cambridge: Cambridge University Press, 1986), 145. Many lawyers in Berlanstein's study of the Toulousan bar could not break into such a glutted system, and, therefore, turned to other pursuits. Editing and compiling were those of Des Essarts.

32. See the conclusion for more on Des Essarts' revolutionary career.

33. Des Essarts, "Discours preliminaire," iv–v.

34. Maza, *Private Lives,* 313.

35. Ibid., 26.

Chapter 2. Domestic Magistracy

1. *Causes célèbres,* 117, case 388 (1784): 86–87.

2. Jean Delumeau, Introduction to "Le Discours des deux réformes" in *Histoire des pères et de la paternité,* eds. Jean Delumeau and Daniel Roche (Paris: Larousse, 1990), 130.

3. See Jeffrey Merrick's discussion of verdicts in eighteenth-century French court cases which checked "despotic" power. "Patriarchalism and Constitutionalism in Eighteenth-Century Parlementary Discourse," *Studies in Eighteenth-Century Culture* 20 (1990): 327.

4. Lynn Hunt, *The Family Romance of the French Revolution* (Berkeley: University of California Press, 1992), 196.

5. *Causes célèbres* 140, case 504 (1786): 97. Case 504 is a continuation of 388.

6. For a recent discussion of the marriage strategies of the nobility, which included marriage into wealthy bourgeois families, see Robert Descimon, "Conflits familiaux dans la robe parisienne aux XVI et XVII siècles," *Cahiers d'histoire* 45 (4), 2000: 677–97. Such practices made the concerns of de Rois somewhat anachronistic, yet these concerns are regularly repeated by litigants in the *Causes célèbres.* The prevalence of intermarriage between noble and commoner is still debated by historians. Gayle Brunelle, in her study of marriages between noblewomen and male commoners, finds that male nobles married "beneath" their rank far less often than female nobles. Building on earlier work by James B. Wood ("Endogamy and *Mésalliance*: the Marriage Patterns of the Nobility of the Election of Bayeaux, 1543–1669," *French Historical Studies* 10 (Spring 1978): 375–92), Brunelle explains that "families considered the lineal descendants of [all sons, not just the eldest], who would bear the family name and noble status, too valuable to risk through even the hint of taint from a non-noble mother." "Dangerous Liaisons: *Mésalliance* and Early Modern French Noblewomen," *French Historical Studies* 19 1 (Spring 1995): 99.

7. *Causes célèbres* 117, case 388 (1784): 18.

8. *Causes célèbres* 140, case 504 (1786): 22.

9. *Causes célèbres*, 125.

10. Twenty-five was the legal age of majority for women; thus Noailles' father's consent was not necessary. De Rois was still a minor, however, thirty being the age of majority for men.

11. Farge, "Familles: L'honneur et le secret," *Histoire de la vie privée*, ed. Roger Chartier, vol. 3 (Paris: Editions du Seuil, 1986), 601.

12. *Causes célèbres* 112, case 367 (1784): 57.

13. *Causes célèbres* 113, case 374 (1784): 159.

14. *Causes célèbres* 140, case 504 (1786): 103.

15. *Causes célèbres* 117, case 388 (1784): 5.

16. *Causes célèbres* 89, case 271 (1782): 198–99.

17. *Causes célèbres* 140, case 504 (1786): 94–95.

18. *Causes célèbres*, 134.

19. *Causes célèbres* 125, case 430 (1785): 178

20. This rhetoric clearly anticipates the stigmatization of celibacy which began with the forbidding of monastic vows in 1790 and continued until under Dechristianization, former priests were required to marry. Jacques Gélis claims that revolutionaries saw celibates as "social parasites," subjected them to a special tax, and barred them from public service. "L'Enfant et l'Evolution de la conception de la vie sous la Révolution," in *L'Enfant, la Famille, et la Révolution Française*, (Paris: Olivier Orban, 1990), 70. For the Enlightenment background to these developments, see Carol Blum, *Strength in Numbers: Population, Reproduction, and Power in Eighteenth-Century France* (Baltimore: Johns Hopkins University Press, 2002).

21. A discussion of Barère's biases follows below in chapter four when he defends a textile worker accused of infanticide.

22. *Causes célèbres* 117, case 388 (1784): 143–44.

23. *Causes célèbres* 140, case 504 (1786), 98.

24. *Causes célèbres* 117, case 388 (1784): 107.

25. *Causes célèbres*, 84.

26. *Causes célèbres* 134, case 485 (1786): 91.

27. Hunt, *The Family Romance*, 65.
28. *Causes célèbres* 140, case 504 (1786): 90.
29. *Causes célèbres* 89, case 271 (1782): 38, 173.
30. *Causes célèbres* 117, case 388 (1784): 6.
31. *Causes célèbres* 140, case 504 (1786): 99.
32. Daumas, 101. Using money for this kind of retribution was common in the seventeenth century as well. According to James Farr: "A primary purpose of the judicial process in cases of rapt came to be the rehabilitation of the honor of the woman or, more accurately, her family. The judges were operating according to the rules of a sexual economy. They conceived of a woman's honor as a commodity with a monetary value pegged to her social station and therefore her marketability in marriage. The litigants, for their part, understood the same rules." *Authority and Sexuality in Early Modern Burgundy* (New York: Oxford University Press, 1995), 102.
33. Quoted by Bernard Schnapper, "Liberté, égalité, autorité: la famille devant les assemblées révolutionnaires (1790–1800)" in *L'Enfant, la Famille, et la Révolution Française*, ed. Michel Vovelle (Paris: Olivier Orban, 1990), 327.
34. Maza, *Private Lives and Public Affairs*, 323.
35. *Causes célèbres* 12, case 30 (1775): 103–4.
36. *Causes célèbres*, 92; 95.
37. *Causes célèbres*, 99.
38. *Causes célèbres*, 101–2.
39. *Causes célèbres*, 105.
40. *Causes célèbres*, 111.
41. *Causes célèbres* 51, case 136 (1779): 183.
42. *Causes célèbres*, 151.
43. *Causes célèbres* (second series) 13, case 70 (1775): 89.
44. *Causes célèbres* 51, case 136 (1779): 171.
45. *Causes célèbres*, 154.
46. *Causes célèbres* 61, case 159 (1780): 147.
47. Garrioch, 65 and Nicole Castan, *Les criminels de Languedoc: les exigences d'ordre et les voies du rèssentiment dans une société pre-révolutionnaire, 1750–1790* (Toulouse: l'Université de Toulouse-le-Mirail, 1980), 179.
48. *Causes célèbres* 42, case 113 (1778), 46–48.
49. *Causes célèbres* 110, case 358 (1784): 52.
50. *Causes célèbres* 51, case 136 (1779): 203–4.
51. *Causes célèbres*, 205–6.
52. *Causes célèbres* 51, case 136 (1779): 190.
53. *Causes célèbres* 54, case 144 (1779): 16.
54. *Causes célèbres* 43, case 113 (1778): 22.
55. *Causes célèbres* 61, case 159 (1780): 73.
56. *Causes célèbres* 148, case 543 (1787): 180–81.

Chapter 3. The Bonds of Matrimony

1. *Causes célèbres* (second series) 10, case 58 (1774): 239.
2. See Lottin and Savelon, p. 125: "According to canon law, the following are

the only precise reasons acknowledged for granting a physical separation or `divortium quo ad thorum': mutual consent for taking religious vows, adultery by one of the spouses, heresy, sorcery, serious brutality and mal-treatment. On the other hand, insanity, illness, or a criminal conviction can invoke the same reasons for demanding a separation, even though in France jurists establish a sexual and social discrimination."

3. *Causes célèbres* 128, case 452 (1785): 171–2. And apparently there were more separations in the late-eighteenth century than ever before. Lottin and Savelon found that "separations were more numerous in the second third of the eighteenth century than in the first. . . . Three-fourths of the requests came from women. Women obviously profited from the right that the Church gave them to initiate requests." Lottin and Savelon, 114.

4. *Causes célèbres* 17, case 39 (1776): 3–4.

5. Lottin, "La couple. . . ," 163.

6. *Causes célèbres* 6, case 40 (1773): 115.

7. *Causes célèbres* 6, case 41 (1773): 191–92.

8. *Causes célèbres* 65, case 171 (1780): 148.

9. *Causes célèbres*, 55.

10. *Causes célèbres*, 158–59.

11. *Causes célèbres*, 118.

12. Merrick, "Domestic Politics," 13.

13. *Causes célèbres* (second series) 10, case 58 (1774): 218–19.

14. *Causes célèbres*, 230.

15. *Causes célèbres*, 243–4.

16. *Causes célèbres* (1771), quoted in Isabelle Vissière, *Procès des femmes au temps des philosophes* (Paris: des Femmes, 1985), 278–79.

17. *Causes célèbres* (second series) 10, case 58 (1774): 240.

18. *Causes célèbres* 82, case 241 (1781): 185.

19. *Causes célèbres* (second series) 6, case 41 (1773): 209–10.

20. *Causes célèbres* 158, case 577 (1788): 110.

21. *Causes célèbres*, 126.

22. *Causes célèbres* 158, case 577 (1788): 164.

23. *Causes célèbres* 5, case 37 (1773): 246–47.

24. *Causes célèbres*, 166–67.

25. In most cases where physical brutality—and even murder—was committed against the wife, the wife's character was investigated as the probable cause of the brutality. In other words, did she deserve his blows? In one case Des Essarts observed: "If this woman had possessed a violent or shrewish temper, one would be less astonished at the conduct of her husband [who beat and eventually murdered her], but she opposed his ferocity with nothing more than tears, sweetness, and patience." *Causes célèbres* 83, case 247 (1781): 191.

26. *Causes célèbres* 6, case 40 (1773): 179–80.

27. *Causes célèbres* 158, case 577 (1788): 172–3.

28. Roderick Phillips, *Putting Asunder: A History of Divorce in Western Society* (Cambridge: Cambridge University Press, 1988), 160–61.

29. *Causes célèbres* 161, case 585 (1788): 56.

30. *Causes célèbres*, 89.

31. *Causes célèbres* 16, case 80 (1774): 123.

32. *Causes célèbres* 28, case 72 (1777): 8–9.
33. *Causes célèbres*, 29.
34. *Causes célèbres* 13, case 32 (1775): 141–42.
35. *Causes célèbres* 28, case 72 (1777): 60.
36. *Causes célèbres*, 15–16.
37. *Causes célèbres*, 102.
38. *Causes célèbres*, 155.
39. *Causes célèbres*, 60.
40. *Causes célèbres* 85, case 257 (1782): 191–92.
41. See Blum, *Strength in Numbers.*
42. *Causes célèbres* 28, case 72 (1777): 145–46.
43. *Causes célèbres* 75, case 197 (1781): 82.
44. *Causes célèbres* 28, case 72 (1777): 30.
45. *Causes célèbres*, 144.
46. *Causes célèbres*, 28; 17.
47. *Causes célèbres*, 60–61.

Chapter 4. Atrocious Prejuices

1. *Causes célèbres* 59, case 155 (1779): 157.
2. *Causes célèbres*, 173.
3. Arlette Farge, "Familles: L'honneur et le secret" in *Histoire de la vie privée*, ed. Roger Chartier, vol. 3 (Paris: Editions du Seuil, 1986), 590.
4. Nicole Castan, "Le public et le particulier" in *Histoire de la vie privée*, 426.
5. Garrioch, 76.
6. The "closeted individual" develops his civility alone, "walled off" from others. See Norbert Elias, *The Civilizing Process* (Oxford University Press, Blackwell, 1994 [1939]), 204.
7. Mona Ozouf, "L'opinion publique," in *The French Revolution and the Creation of Modern Political Culture*, vol. 1: *The Political Culture of the Old Regime*, ed. Keith Michael Baker (New York: Pergamon, 1987), 423. See also Arlette Farge, *Dire et mal dire: L'opinion publique au XVIIIe siècle* (Paris: Editions du Seuil, 1992) which attempts to restore to the "people" an active role in the construction and functioning of the "public sphere."
8. Keith Michael Baker, *Inventing the French Revolution* (Cambridge: Cambridge University Press, 1990), 172.
9. Roger Chartier, "Culture populaire et culture politique dans l'Ancien Régime: quelques réflexions," in *The French Revolution and the Creation of Modern Political Culture*, ed. Keith Michael Baker, vol.1 (New York: Pergamon, 1987), 245.
10. This genesis of the public is perhaps ironic, given the role that aristocratic women played in the salons. See Dena Goodman: "In an age of Enlightenment embodied in public opinion, the policing function of the salonnière seemed unnecessary and thus despotic." *The Republic of Letters: a Cultural History of the Enlightenment* (Ithaca: Cornell University Press, 1994), 235.
11. *Causes célèbres*, 164; 167.
12. *Causes célèbres*, 91.
13. *Causes célèbres* 107, case 349 (1783): 183, 184–85.

14. This form of individualism was more characteristic of English definitions of citizenship; Jacobins argued for a more collective definition and thus were ambivalent about the "homo clausus." Higonnet, 135.
15. *Causes célèbres* 90, case 275 (1782): 166.
16. *Causes célèbres* 121, case 401 (1785): 4.
17. *Causes célèbres* 75, case 198 (1781): 106–7.
18. *Causes célèbres* 106, case 344 (1783): 12.
19. *Causes célèbres* 75, case 198 (1781): 108–9.
20. Castan, *Les criminels,* 175.
21. *Causes célèbres,* 111.
22. *Causes célèbres,* 116.
23. *Causes célèbres,* 115.
24. Vissière, 122.
25. *Causes célèbres* 113.
26. Failure to make a declaration would leave her subject to capital punishment should the infant be stillborn, according to the law of 1556 mandating "declarations de grossesse" by unwed pregnant women. Considering infanticide a form of parricide, the law presumed that concealment led to premeditated murder: thus, the unregistered dead baby was by definition a murder victim.
27. *Causes célèbres* 121, case 401 (1785): 7.
28. *Causes célèbres,* 10.
29. *Causes célèbres* 75, case 198 (1781): 121–22.
30. *Causes célèbres* 132, case 474 (1785): 87–88.
31. *Causes célèbres* 116, case 387 (1784): 185–86.
32. A fact amply attested to in Julius Ruff, *Violence in Early Modern Europe, 1500–1800* (Cambridge: Cambridge University Press, 2001) and Georges Vigarello, *A History of Rape in France* (New York: Polity, 2001).
33. Farr, *Authority and Sexuality,* 108–9.
34. Olwen Hufton, *The Poor of Eighteenth-Century France, 1750–1789* (Oxford University Press, 1974), 324.
35. See Tracey Rizzo, "'Between Dishonor and Death': Infanticides in the *Causes célèbres* of Eighteenth-century France," *Women's History Review* 2004, 13 (1): 5–22.
36. *Causes célèbres* 81, case 234 (1781), 79.
37. *Causes célèbres* 156, case 570 (1787): 119.
38. *Causes célèbres,* 130–31.
39. *Causes célèbres,* 83.
40. *Causes célèbres,* 76
41. *Causes célèbres,* 132.
42. *Causes célèbres* 4, case 22 (1773), 156–57.
43. *Causes célèbres,* 1, case 2 (1775), 159–69. Note that due to editorial changes made two years after its inception in 1773, the *Causes* began numbering again at 1 in 1775.
44. *Causes célèbres* 140, case 511 (1787), 188–89.
45. 139/501/97:
46. Appending relevant literature was not unique to this case. Depending on the case, Des Essarts would often indulge his readers in long digressions which considered the implications of certain legal or medical questions. At the end of

one case, for example, wherein a woman was convicted of having poisoned her husband, Des Essarts included a brochure entitled: "What irrefutable signs can be found in sick or dead bodies which indicate to a doctor that a man has been poisoned by a corrosive when it is necessary to inform the judges about the crime?" (*Causes célèbres* 112, case 369 (1784): 173.) Other issues were sources for such digressions as well. Lüsebrink sums these up: "The ambition to respond to his readers' needs for information and knowledge can equally be found at the base of digressions concerning judicial medicine, public economy, the construction of shelters for illegitimate children, the repression of prostitution among different peoples since antiquity through the eighteenth century, inserted in the accounts of affairs including respectively murder, fraudulent bankruptcy, infanticide, and prostitution. One discovers in the other texts of the *Causes célèbres* observations concerning balloons and lightning rods, critical remarks on the increasing rural exodus and urban luxury, very general considerations on contemporary pedagogy, beside his position on the problem of slavery and the treatment of blacks." Lüsebrink, "Les répresentations," 153.

47. *Causes célèbres* 85, case 257 (1782): 200.

48. Those currently in existence were already overloaded. François Lebrun reports that in Paris, for example, in 1762 a record high number of infants were placed at the "couche de Paris": 7676, or more than 1/3 of all baptisms that year. Lebrun, *La vie conjugal sous l'ancien regime* (Paris: Armand Colin, 1975), 155.

49. *Causes célèbres* 85, case 257 (1782): 199–200.

50. *Causes célèbres* 147, case 540 (1787): 192.

51. Rousseau, *Oeuvres complètes*, vol. 3, ed. Michel Launay: "Emile" (Paris, 1967–71), 247. Quoted in *Women, the Family and Freedom*, vol. 1, ed. Susan Groag Bell and Karen Offen (Stanford: Stanford University Press, 1983), 49.

52. Renewal was personified by the breast-feeding mother, more likely to be a poor woman like those described here, whose incorruptible milk strengthened the family and the nation. The use of this metaphor of renewal is described by Mary L. Jacobus, "Incorruptible Milk: Breast-feeding and the French Revolution," in *Rebel Daughters: Women and the French Revolution*, eds. Sara E. Melzer and Leslie W. Rabine (New York: Oxford University Press, 1992): 54–75.

Conclusion

1. Des Essarts, *Procès Fameux jugés depuis la Révolution* vol. 11 (Paris: by the Author, An 7): 133.

2. Keith Michael Baker, *Inventing the French Revolution* (Cambridge: Cambridge University Press, 1990) 172.

3. *Causes célèbres* 173, case 616 (1789): 40, 119.

4. Girondins, or Girondists, were a group of deputies from Southwestern France, the Gironde, who served in the Legislative Assembly (1791–92) and the Convention (1792–93). They differed from the Jacobins on key questions like the pursuit of a pre-emptive war and the fate of the King. They were purged because of "moderatism." See note 8, below.

5. Des Essarts, "Introduction" to *La vie et les crimes de Robespierre et de ses principaux complices, avec le détail des circonstances qui ont accompagné leur supplice* (Paris, 1797).

6. *Procès fameux*, 134-5.
7. Ibid., 138.
8. Quoted in Mona Ozouf, "Girondins," in *A Critical Dictionary of the French Revolution*, eds François Furet and Mona Ozouf; trans. Arthur Goldhammer (Cambridge and London: Harvard University Press, 1989), 354.
9. *Procès fameux*, 140.
10. Ibid., "Charlotte Corday," 34–35.
11. Ibid., 146.
12. Manon Roland, quoted by Des Essarts, *Procès fameux*, 147.
13. Ibid., 145.
14. Ibid., 147, 148.
15. See Higonnet, 92–93.
16. Thomas, 80.

Bibliography

Baker, Keith. *Inventing the French Revolution.* Cambridge: Cambridge University Press, 1990.

Bell, David. *The Cult of the Nation in France: Inventing Nationalism, 1680–1800.* Cambridge: Harvard University Press, 2003.

———. *Lawyers and Citizens: The Making of a Political Elite in Old Regime France.* New York: Oxford University Press, 1994.

———. "Lawyers and Politics in Eighteenth-Century Paris." Diss. Princeton U., 1991.

Benabou, Erica. *La prostitution et la police des moeurs au XVIIIè siècle.* Paris: Librairie Académique Perrin, 1987.

Bérenguier, Nadine. "Fiction dans les archives: Adultère et stratégies de défense dans deux mémoires judiciaires au XVIIIe siècle." *Studies on Voltaire and the Eighteenth Century* 308 (1993): 257–79.

Berlanstein, Lenard R. *The Barristers of Toulouse in the 18th Century (1740–1793).* Baltimore: Johns Hopkins University Press, 1975.

Blum, Carol. *Rousseau and the Republic of Virtue.* Ithaca: Cornell University Press, 1986.

———. *Strength in Numbers: Population, Reproduction, and Power in Eighteenth-Century France.* Baltimore: Johns Hopkins University Press, 2002.

Bologne, Jean-Claude. *Histoire de la pudeur.* Paris: O. Orban, 1988.

Bonnet, Jean-Claude. "De la famille à la patrie." *Histoire des Pères et de la Paternité.* Edited by Jean Delameau and Daniel Roche, Paris: Larousse, 1990. 235–58.

Brooks, Peter. *The Melodramatic Imagination.* New Haven: Yale University Press, 1976.

Brunelle, Gayle. "Dangerous Liaisons: *Mésalliance* and Early Modern French Noblewomen." *French Historical Studies* 19 1 (Spring 1995): 75–103.

Canovan, Margaret. "Rousseau's Two Concepts of Citizenship." In *Women in Western Political Philosophy.* Edited by Ellen Kennedy and Susan Mendus, 78–105. New York: St. Martin's, 1987. 78–105.

Carbonnier, Jean. "Le statut de l'enfant en droit civil pendant la Révolution." *L'Enfant, la Famille, et la Révolution Française.* Edited by Michel Vovelle, 297–306. Paris: Olivier Orban, 1990.

Carbonnier-Burkard, Marianne. "Les variations protestants." *Histoire des pères et de la paternité.* Edited by Jean Delumeau and Daniel Roche, 155–78. Paris: Larousse, 1990.

Castan, Nicole. "Le public et le particulier." *Histoire de la vie privée.* Edited by Roger Chartier, 413–54, vol. 3. Paris: Seuil, 1986.

———. *Les criminels de Languedoc: les exigences d'ordre et les voies du réssentiment dans une société pre-révolutionnaire, 1750–1790.* Toulouse: l'Université de Toulouse-le-Mirail, 1980.

———. "Les femmes devant la justice: Toulouse, XVIIIe siècle." *Femmes et pouvoirs sous l'ancien régime.* Edited by Danielle Haase Dubosc and Eliane Viennot, 276–84. Paris: Rivages/Histoire, 1991.

———. *Vivre ensemble.* Paris: Gallimard/Julliard, 1981.

Chartier, R., J. Molino, et al. *L'interprétation de textes.* Paris: Minuit, 1989.

Chartier, Roger. "Culture populaire et culture politique dans l'Ancien Régime: quelques réflexions." *The French Revolution and the Creation of Modern Political Culture.* Edited by Keith Michael Baker, 243–58, vol. 1. New York: Pergamon, 1987.

———. *The Cultural Uses of Print in Early Modern France.* Translated by Lydia G. Cochrane. Princeton: Princeton University Press, 1987.

———. "Introduction." *Histoire de la vie privée,* Edited by Roger Chartier, 22–25, vol. 3. Paris: Seuil, 1986.

———. *Lectures et lecteurs dans l'ancienne France.* Paris: Seuil, 1987.

Conner, Susan. "Public Virtue and Public Women: Prostitution in Revolutionary Paris, 1793–1794." *Eighteenth-Century Studies* 28.2 (1994–1995): 221–40.

Corbin, Alain, ed. *Violences sexuelles.* Paris: Imago, 1989.

Cummings, Mark. "Elopement, Family and the Courts: the Crime of `Rapt' in Early Modern France," *Proceedings of the Annual Meeting of the Western Society for French History* 4 (1976): 118–25.

Darnton, R. and D. Roche, eds. *Revolution in Print: The Press in France, 1775–1800.* Berkeley: University of California Press, 1989.

Daumas, M. *L'Affaire d'Esclans: conflits familiaux au XVIIIè siècle.* Paris: Seuil, 1987.

Dauphin, Christine and Arlette Farge, et al. "Culture et pouvoir des femmes: essai d'historiographie."*Annales: Economies, Societies, Civilizations* 41.2 (March-April 1986): 271–93.

Delumeau, Jean. Introduction to "le Discours des deux réformes." *Histoire des pères et de la paternité.* Edited by Jean Delumeau and Daniel Roche, 129–30. Paris: Larousse, 1990.

Depauw, Jacques. "Illicit Sexual Activity and Society in Eighteenth-century Nantes." *Family and Society, Selections from "Annales: Economies, Societies, Civilizations."* Edited by Robert Forster and Orest Ranum. Translated by Elborg Forster and Patricia M. Ranum, 145–91. Baltimore: Johns Hopkins University Press, 1976.

Des Essarts, Nicolas Toussaint le Moyne. *Les causes célèbres, curieuses et intéressantes de toutes les cours souveraines du Royaume avec les jugements qui les ont decidées.* Paris, 1773–89. 98 vols.

———. "Discours préliminaire." *Essai sur l'Histoire général des Tribunaux des peuples, tant anciens que modernes.* Paris, 1778.

———. "Emile et Sophie, ou les époux désunis." Paris: Nyon, 1784.

———. *Procès fameux: Extraits de l'essai sur l'historie générale des tribunaux des peuples.* Paris, 1786–90. 29 vols.

———. *Procès fameux jugés depuis la Révolution.* Paris, Ans 7–10.

———. "Réponse de N.T le Moyne Des Essarts, homme de la loi et électeur du département de Paris à ses calomniateurs." Paris, 1790?

———. *La vie et les crimes de Robespierre et de ses principaux complices, avec le détail des circonstances qui ont accompagné leur supplice.* Paris, 1797.

Descimon, Robert, "Conflits familiaux dans la robe parisienne aux XVI et XVII siècles," *Cahiers d'histoire* 45 (4), 2000: 677–97.

Donzelot, Jacques. *The Policing of Families.* Translated by Robert Hurley. New York: Pantheon, 1979.

Duncan, Carol. "Happy Mothers and Other New Ideas in French Art." *Art Bulletin* 55 (1973): 70–83.

Elias, Norbert. *The Civilizing Process.* Translated by Edmund Jephcott. New York: Urizen, 1982.

———. *The Court Society.* Translated by Edmund Jephcott. Oxford: Blackwell, 1983

Esmein, A. *Histoire de la procedure criminelle en France.* Paris, 1882. Rpt. Liechtenstein: Vaduz Reprints, 1978.

Fairchilds, Cissie. "Female Sexual Attitudes and the Rise of Illegitimacy." *Journal of Interdisciplinary History* 8 (Spring 1978): 627–67.

Farge, Arlette, ed. *Affaires de sang.* Paris: Imago, 1988.

———. *Dire et mal dire: L'opinion publique au XVIIIe siècle.* Paris: Editions du Seuil, 1992.

———. "Familles: L'honneur et le secret." *Histoire de la vie privée.* Edited by Roger Chartier, 581–617, vol. 3. Paris: Editions du Seuil, 1986.

———. "L'Histoire ebruitée: des femmes dans la société pre-révolutionnaire Parisienne." *L'Histoir sans qualités.* Edited by Christiane Dufranctel. Paris: Galilée, 1979. 15–39.

———. "Introduction." *Le miroir des femmes,* 11–82. Paris: Montalba, 1982.

———. *La vie fragile: violence, pouvoirs et solidarités à Paris au XVIIIè siècle.* Paris: Hachette, 1986.

———. *Vivre dans la rue à Paris au XVIIIè siècle.* Paris: Gallimard, 1979.

Farge, Arlette and Michel Foucault. *Le désordre des familles.* Paris: Gallimard, 1982.

Farr, James. *Authority and Sexuality in Early Modern Burgundy.* New York: Oxford, 1995.

———. "The Pure and Disciplined Body: Hierarchy, Morality, and Symbolism in France during the Catholic Reformation." *Journal of Interdisciplinary History* 21 (1991): 391–415.

Faurè, Christine. *Democracy Without Women: Feminism and the Rise of Liberal Individualism in France.* Translated by Claudia Gorbman and John Berks. Bloomington: University of Indiana Press, 1991.

Fitzsimmons, Michael. *The Parisian Order of Barristers and the French Revolution.* Cambridge: Harvard University Press, 1987.

Flandrin, Jean-Louis. *Families in Former Times.* Translated by Richard Southern. Cambridge: Cambridge University Press, 1979.

———. "Repression and Change in the Sexual Life of Young People in Medieval and Early Modern Times." *Family and Sexuality in French History.* Edited by Robert Wheaton and Tamara K. Hareven. Philadelphia: University of Pennsylvania Press, 1980. 27–48.

Fouquet, Catherine. *La femme au temps de la Révolution.* Paris: Stock/C. Pernoud, 1989.

Fouquet, Catherine and Knibiehler, Yvonne. *La femme et les médecins: Analyse historique.* Paris: Hachette, 1983.

Fraisse, Genvieve. "Rupture révolutionnaire et l'histoire des femmes." *Femmes et pouvoirs sous l'ancien régime.* Edited by Danielle Haase Dubosc and Eliane Viennot, 291–305. Paris: Rivages/Histoire, 1991.

Garnot, Benoit. *Un crime conjugal au XVIIIe siècle.* Paris: Imago, 1993.

Garrioch, David. *Neighbourhood and Community in Paris, 1740–1790.* Cambridge: Cambridge University Press, 1986.

Gelbart, Nina Rattner. *Feminine and Opposition Journalism in Old Regime France.* Berkeley: University of California Press, 1987.

Gélis, Jacques. "L'Enfant et l'Evolution de la conception de la vie sous la Révolution." *L'Enfant, la Famille, et la Révolution Française.* Edited by Michel Vovelle, 69–78. Paris: Olivier Orban, 1990.

Gershoy, Leo. *Barère de Vieuzac: A Reluctant Terrorist.* Princeton: Princeton University Press, 1962.

Ghestin, Jacques. "L'action des parlements contre les `mesalliances' au XVIIè et XVIIIè siècles." *Revue Historique de Droit Français et Etranger* 4th Ser. 34 (1956): 197–218.

Goodman, Dena. *The Republic of Letters: a Cultural History of the Enlightenment.* Ithaca: Cornell University Press, 1994.

Grimmer, Claude. *La femme et le bâtard: Amours illégitimes et secrets dans l'Ancienne France.* Paris: Presses de la Rénaissance, 1983.

Habermas, Jürgen. *The Structural Transformation of the Public Sphere.* Translated by Thomas Burger. Cambridge: MIT Press, 1989.

Hanley, Sara. "Engendering the State: Family Formation and State Building in Early Modern France." *French Historical Studies* 16 (January 1989): 4–27.

Higonnet, Patrice. *Goodness Beyond Virtue: Jacobins During the French Revolution* Cambridge: Harvard University Press, 1998.

Hufton, Olwen. *Women and the Limits of Citizenship in the French Revolution.* Toronto: University of Toronto Press, 1992.

———. "Women, Work, and Marriage in Eighteenth-Century France." *Marriage and Society: Studies in the Social History of Marriage.* Edited by R. B. Outhwaite, 186–203. New York: St. Martin's, 1981.

Hunt, Lynn. *The Family Romance of the French Revolution.* Berkeley: University of California Press, 1992.

———. "Introduction: History, Culture, and Text." *The New Cultural History.* Edited by Lynn Hunt, 1–12. Berkeley: University of California Press, 1989.

———. "The Many Bodies of Marie Antoinette: Political Pornography and the Problem of the Feminine in the French Revolution." *Eroticism and the Body Politic.* Edited by Lynn Hunt, 108–30. Baltimore: Johns Hopkins University Press, 1991.

———. *Politics, Culture and Class in the French Revolution.* Berkeley: University of California Press, 1984.

Jacobus, Mary L. "Incorruptible Milk: Breast-feeding and the French Revolution." *Rebel Daughters: Women and the French Revolution.* Edited by Sara E. Melzer and Leslie W. Rabine, 54–75. New York: Oxford University Press, 1992.

Juratic, Sabine. "Contraits conjugales et violences féminines: Epouses meurtrières aux XVIIIème siècle." *Pénélope* 6 (1982): 104–108.

Landes, Joan. *Women and the Public Sphere in the Age of the French Revolution.* Ithaca: Cornell University Press, 1988.

———. "Representing the Body Politic: The Paradox of Gender in the Graphic Politics of the French Revolution." *Rebel Daughters: Women and the French Revolution.* Edited by Sara E. Melzer and Leslie W. Rabine, 15–37. New York: Oxford University Press, 1992.

———. *Visualizing the Nation: Gender, Representation, and Revolution in Eighteenth-Century.* Ithaca: Cornell UP: 2003.

Lebrun, François. *La vie conjugale sous l'ancien regime.* Paris: Armand Colin, 1975.

LeGates, Marlene. "The Cult of Womanhood in Eighteenth-Century Thought." *Eighteenth-Century Studies,* 10 (1976): 21–32.

Lequenne, Michel. "Madame Roland." *Cahiers du féminisme,* 52 (Printemps 1990): 38–40.

Lottin, Alain. "Le couple et sa désagrégation." *La désunion du couple sous l'Ancien Regime: l'Example du nord.* Edited by Alain Lottin, 149–80. Paris: Editions universitaires, 1975.

———. "Naissances illégitimes et filles-mères à Lille." *Revue d'Histoire moderne et contemporaine* 17 (April-June 1970): 278–302.

Lottin, Alain and G. Savelon, "Les Divorcés." *La désunion du couple sous l'Ancien Regime: l'Example du nord.* Edited by Alain Lottin, 113–36. Paris: Editions universitaires, 1975.

Lüsebrink, Hans. "L'Affaire Clêreaux (Rouen 1785–90): Affrontements ideologiques et tensions institutionelles sur la scène judiciaire de la fin du dix-huitème siècle." *Studies on Voltaire and the Eighteenth Century* 191 (1980): 892–900.

———. "Les crimes sexuelles dans les *Causes célèbres.*" *Dix-huitième Siècle* 12 (1980): 153–62.

———. "L'Innocence persécutée et ses avocats: Rhétorique et impact public du discours `sensible' dans la France du XVIIIe siècle." *Revue d'histoire moderne et contemporaine* 40 (1993): 86–101.

———. "Les répresentations sociales de la criminalité en France au XVIIIè siècle." Diss. Ecole des Hautes Etudes en Sciences Sociales, 1983.

Machuelle, J.R. "Séducteurs, volages, et infidèles." *La désunion du couple sous l'Ancien Regime.* Edited by Alain Lottin, 97–112. Paris: Editions universitaires, 1975.

May, Gita. *Madame Roland and the Age of Revolution.* New York: Columbia University Press, 1970.

Maza, Sara. "Domestic Melodrama as Political Ideology: the case of the Comte de Sanois." *American Historical Review* 94 (December 1989): 1249–1265.

———. "Le Tribunal de la nation: les mémoires judiciaires et opinion publique à la fin de l'Ancienne Regime." *Annales: Economies, Societies, Civilizations* 42.1 (January-February, 1987): 73–90.

———. *Private Lives and Public Affairs: The Causes Célèbres of Prerevolutionary France.* Berkeley: University of California Press, 1993.

———. "The Rose-Girl of Salency: Representations of Virtue in Pre-Revolutionary France." *Eighteenth-Century Studies* 22 (Spring 1989): 395–412.

Merrick, Jeffrey. "Conscience and Citizenship in Eighteenth-Century France." *Eighteenth-Century Studies* 21 (Fall 1987): 48–70.

———. Domestic Politics: Divorce and Despotism in Eighteenth-Century France" in *The Past as Prologue: ASECS at Twenty-Five.* Edited by Carla Hay and Sydney Conger, 373–386. New York: AMS Press, 1995.

———. "Fathers and Kings: Patriarchalism and Absolutism in Eighteenth-Century French Politics," *Studies on Voltaire and the Eighteenth Century* 308 (1993): 281–303.

———. "Patriarchalism and Constitutionalism in Eighteenth-Century Parlementary Discourse," *Studies in Eighteenth-Century Culture* 20 (1990): 317–30.

Ozouf, Mona. "L'opinion publique." *The French Revolution and the Creation of Modern Political Culture.* Edited by Keith Michael Baker, 419–34, vol. 1. New York: Pergamon, 1987.

Pateman, Carole. *The Sexual Contract.* Stanford: Stanford University Press, 1988.

Phan, M.C. "Les déclarations de grossese en France (16è–18è siècles)." *Revue d'Histoire moderne et contemporaine* 22 (1975): 61–88.

Phillips, Roderick. "The Attack on Celibacy in Eighteenth-Century France." *Proceedings of the Annual Meeting of the Western Society for French History.* 17 (1990): 165–171.

———. *Putting Asunder: A History of Divorce in Western Society.* Cambridge: Cambridge University Press, 1988.

———. "Women and Family Breakdown in Eighteenth-Century France: Rouen, 1780–1800." *Social History* 2 (May 1976): 197–218.

Proctor, Candice E. *Women, Equality, and the French Revolution.* New York: Greenwood, 1990.

Rizzo, Tracey. "'A Lascivious Climate': Representations of Colonial Subjectivity in the *Causes célèbres* of Eighteenth-century France." *Journal of Carribean History* 2000, 34 (1–2): 157–77.

———. "'Between Dishonor and Death': Infanticides in the *Causes célèbres* of Eighteenth-century France." *Women's History Review* 2004, 13 (1): 5–21.

Ronsin, Francis. *Le contrat sentimental: Débats sur le mariage, l'amour, le divorce, de l'Ancien Régime à la Restauration.* Paris: Aubier, 1990.

———. "Le divorce révolutionnaire." *L'Enfant, la Famille, et la Révolution Française.* Edited by Michel Vovelle, 307–24. Paris: Olivier Orban, 1990.

Rousseau, Jean-Jacques. *Oeuvres complètes.* Edited by Bernard Gagnebin and Marcel Raymond. Paris: Pléiade, 1969. 4 vols.

Ruff, Julius, R. *Crime, Justice, and Public Order in Old Regime France.* London: Croom Helm, 1984.

———. *Violence in Early Modern Europe, 1500–1800.* Cambridge: Cambridge University Press, 2001.

Schnapper, Bernard. "Liberté, égalité, autorité: la famille devant les assemblées révolutionnaires (1790–1800)." *L'Enfant, la Famille, et la Révolution Française.* Edited by Michel Vovelle, 325–340. Paris: Olivier Orban, 1990.

Scott, Joan Wallach. *Only Paradoxes to Offer: French Feminists and the Rights of Man.* Cambridge: Harvard University Press, 1996.

Sgard, Jean. "La litterature des causes célèbres." *Approches des Lumières: Mélanges offerts à Jean Fabre.* Edited by Bernard Guyon, 459–70. Paris: Klinksieck, 1974.

Shovlin, John. "Toward a Reinterpretation of Revolutionary Anti-Nobilism: The Political Economy of Honor in the Old Regime." *Journal of Modern History* 72 1 (2000): 35–66.

Singham, Shanti. "Bewtixt Cattle and Men: Jews, Blacks, and Women, and the Declaration of the Rights of Man," in *The French Idea of Freedom.* Edited by Dale Van Kley, 114–53. Stanford: Stanford, 1994.

Smith, Jay. *The Culture of Merit.* Ann Arbor: University of Michigan Press, 1996.

Sonnet, Martine. *L'éducation de filles au temps des Lumières.* Paris: Cerf, 1987.

———. "Les leçons paternelles." *Histoire des Pères et de la Paternité.* Edited by Jean Delameau and Daniel Roche, 259–278. Paris: Larousse, 1990.

Spencer, Samia, ed. *French Women and the Age of Enlightenment.* Bloomington: Indiana University Press, 1984.

Swiderski, Marie. "L'amour interdit ou la femme entre `nature' et conditions feminines." *Aimer en France, 1760–1860.* Edited by Jean Erhard and Paul Viallaneix, 147–158. Clermont-Ferrand: Association des publications de la Faculté des Lettres et Sciences humaines. 1980.

Thomas, Chantal. "Heroism in the Feminine: The Examples of Charlotte Corday and Madame Roland," *Eighteenth Century Theory and Interpretation:* (Special Issue) 30, 1989: 67–82.

Traer, James. *Marriage and the Family in Eighteenth-Century France.* Ithaca: Cornell University Press, 1983.

Vigarello, Georges. *A History of Rape in France,* New York. Polity, 2001.

Vila, Anne C. *Enlightenment and Pathology.* Baltimore: Johns Hopkins, University Press, 1998.

Vissière, Isabelle. *Procès des femmes au temps des philosophes.* Paris: des Femmes, 1985.

Vovelle, Michel. "L'enfance et la famille dans la Révolution française." *L'Enfant, la Famille, et la Révolution française.* Edited by Marie-Françoise Lévy, 13–24. Paris: Olivier Orban, 1989.

Watt, Jeffrey. *The Making of Modern Marriage: Matrimonial Control and the Rise of Sentiment in Neuchâtel, 1550–1800.* Ithaca: Cornell University Press, 1992.

Wood, James B. "Endogamy and *Mésalliance*: the Marriage Patterns of the Nobility of the Election of Bayeaux, 1543–1669," *French Historical Studies* 10 (Spring 1978): 375–92.

Index